The Soul of Grove City College:

A Personal View

By L. John Van Til

Front Cover Photo: "Jesus Teaching." From inside Harbison Chapel at Grove City College.

Back Cover Top Photo: "Board of Trustees 1895." From inside Harbison Chapel at Grove City College.

Back Cover Bottom Photo: "College Seal 1884." From inside Harbison Chapel at Grove City College.

Pine Grove Publishing, 2015

ISBN-13: 978-1508954507
ISBN-10: 150895450X

Copyright © 2015 L. John Van Til

Requests for information and bulk orders should be emailed to: GCCsoul@gmail.com

All rights reserved. No part of this publication may be reproduced, stored in a retrieval system, or transmitted in any form or by any means—electronic, mechanical, photocopy, recording, or any other—except by brief quotations for printed reviews, without the prior permission of the publisher.

Photos: Daniel Peiffer

This book is dedicated with much love to

Kathryn Anne Van Til

my

wife, editor, and intellectual companion

Acknowledgements

Writing books always requires more insight and effort than the author is able to muster to reach the goal—a finished book. This one is no different, even though it is a "personal view" and limited to one main theme in the College's history—its spiritual life. I wish to note here those who have contributed to the gestation, development, and writing of this book. And, it is with profound thanks that I do so.

Even though this book is dedicated to her, I gratefully acknowledge the contributions my Kathryn Anne has made in creating this book. Since part of this book is about our personal experience with J. Howard Pew and then decades as part of the College community, Kathryn has been fully involved in this experience. Thus, as the writing began, we had good times reliving many of the experiences written about here.

Next, I wish to acknowledge the special role played in this effort by several friends and colleagues. A principal person in getting this book off the ground was Dr. James Thrasher. For at least a decade, Jim would say frequently to me or my wife, "When are you going to write that book about the College?" Actually, he cajoled, urged, and then encouraged the effort. I think he recognized that I was the last man standing who personally knew J. Howard Pew well and that I was a member of the faculty which created the rel/phil course. Thanks, Jim.

From another angle, special recognition goes to Dr. W. Andrew Hoffecker. We met on the third floor of Crawford Hall as we both settled into our offices as newly appointed faculty members in the summer of 1972. Instantly, we recognized that we were cut from the same cloth—Biblical Christians interested in intellectual history and theology. For years we worked together on the College curriculum, especially in creating the rel/phil course. After he left and spent many years teaching in the Reformed Seminary, we renewed our bonds and have continued our spiritual, intellectual, and social ties. I especially appreciate Andy's reading this book in manuscript form since he was part of it for years. His reading resulted in suggestions and definitions that only he could make. I thank you with more than words. I must add that Dr. Hoffecker has become a leading Christian scholar with focus on church history. He is recognized far and wide in the Christian community.

As noted in the text, Ross Foster and I met after the first fall faculty convocation in 1972, at a faculty coffee in the Assistant Dean of Men's home on campus. We, too, became intellectual and spiritual soul-mates, having also been cut from the same cloth and having studied in the same tradition. We also became close social friends. It was in this context that we learned continuously about the challenges he faced as Dean of Students and later as Vice President for Student Affairs. Only some of the challenges he faced are recounted in the text. Indeed, it would take a substantial volume to cover even a modest number of them. And, one more point about Ross. Those of us who worked with him in forming the rel/phil course will always remember his contribution in the field of epistemology (the problem of knowledge). He has written many fine pieces in this area and they ought to be collected and published. Thanks, Ross, for reading the manuscript and for being a good friend.

Everyone associated with the College knows how important John Sparks has been to the institution for more than a half-century, that is, since his student days to this very hour. I met John when President MacKenzie invited me down to the boardroom to meet a faculty candidate. It was John Sparks. He was hired and by the fall we were on our way to becoming life-long friends, colleagues, and even business partners. He, too, came with the same worldview as that held by Hoffecker and Foster. Many of his wonderful qualities are set out in the text, but I want to add here my gratitude for his loyalty and decades-long friendship, including encouragement in my writing.

Lee Wishing of the College's Center for Vision & Values has encouraged the writing of this book, too. But more. We have become intellectual and spiritual companions as we have worked together for 10 years at the Center. I admire Lee's continuous effort to grow in knowledge and understanding of a Christian worldview. He also took time to read the manuscript of this book, making solid suggestions. Thank you, Lee.

My son, Seth Jon, the College's Director of Safety and Security, spent time examining township and county records in the areas around Grove City, looking for data on Isaac Ketler. From time to time he visited local rural churches and adjacent graveyards as he gathered information. Thank you, Seth. I also thank my daughter-in-law, Heidi Van Til, who happily reads most of what I write, making thoughtful, encouraging comments. A long-time friend, now in heaven, historian Dr. David Armour is thought of frequently for his encouraging words to write down this spiritual journey.

Terry Thomas and Andy Toncic spent time with me by phone or in person as they commented on facets of the College's 1970s and 1980s. They were students and then served in Student Affairs. They are responsible for contributing some of the "color" found in the text. Thank you, Terry and Andy.

In addition to years of working among College records stored in nooks and crannies on the campus, recently I have had the benefit of College Archivist Hilary Walczak's great memory and research skills in tracking down elusive items. Thanks, Hilary.

In June 2014, retired President MacKenzie made time for me to visit for an afternoon and evening in his apartment in New Wilmington, PA. We reminisced about the old days and his view of numerous issues in his administration. Interestingly, he remembered that I was the first new faculty member that he hired. I thank him for taking time to visit with me. Also, Board Chairman David R. Rathburn's interest in College history and its founders has also been a motivation.

Finally, I wish to give Robert Rider, of the Center for Vision & Values, special thanks for his magnificent help in assembling this book. Indeed, special thanks is also due Robert for shepherding the manuscript through the publication process. His skills and cheerfulness are exceptional.

Table of Contents

Foreword   Page 9
Prologue   Page 11

Chapter 1: My Interest in the Soul of the College
                                              Page 19
Chapter 2: The Source of the College's Soul
                                              Page 37
Chapter 3: A Time of Challenges: Weir Ketler's
    Presidency (1916-1956)
                                              Page 62
Chapter 4: Stanley Harker Welcomes Modernity
    (1956-1971): Spiritual and Otherwise
                                              Page 87
Chapter 5: "Gentlemen, We are Going to Recapture
    Our Christian Principles."
                                              Page 105
Chapter 6: Meeting the Challenge of Student
    Social Life in the MacKenzie Era
                                              Page 129
Chapter 7: An Assemblage of Miscellaneous
    Stories Touching Student Affairs
                                              Page 155

Epilogue   Page 163
Appendix A: Presidents and Board   Page 166
Appendix B: 1877 Catalogue   Page 168
Appendix C: 1921 Campus Standards   Page 191
Appendix D: *The Pilgrims*   Page 208
Appendix E: Photos   Page 213

Index   Page 217
Bibliographic Essay   Page 220

Foreword

Church-related colleges flourished in mid-twentieth century America. But the 1960s witnessed dramatic changes as campus after campus succumbed to the rising tide of secularism in both intellectual worldview and student behavior.

L. John Van Til's *The Soul of Grove City College* tells the powerful story of perhaps the only college which recovered its spiritual roots as the 1970s unfolded. An enlightening read of Grove City College's founders' original vision, its decline and its rebirth.

W. Andrew Hoffecker
Emeritus Professor of Church History
Reformed Theological Seminary

Intellectual History Begins Here:

"Cast down vain imaginations and everything that exalts itself against the knowledge of God, bringing your thoughts captive and obedient to the mind of Christ."
(II Cor. 10:3 ff.)

Soli Deo Gloria

Prologue

People have souls—the life-giving, animating force that sets them apart from other creatures. By analogy, it seems that institutions have souls as well—a set of assumptions, ideas, customs, and practices that define and drive the institution. This seems to be the case with academic institutions like colleges, especially those who have a mission to provide graduates with a Christian perspective on their world and lives.

The point of this essay is to show that Grove City College may be best understood in this way because of certain unique elements in its founding and development. As will be demonstrated, the conception, gestation, birth, and maturing of Grove City College were the result of efforts by a relatively small number of people throughout its history. Further, these pillars of the College were intimately bound together by a deep commitment to a singular view of the world. The principal family names are well known to the College community—the Pews and the Ketlers. What needs to be better known today is the content of their worldview.

Writers on the history of the College have called attention to it, noting time and again how deeply devoted these leaders were to the Presbyterian tradition and its theology. That is to say, they were referring to the Biblical worldview as the backbone of Pew's and Ketler's thinking. And, if one proposition was at the heart of this tradition, one that could often be found on the lips of Joseph Newton Pew, Isaac Ketler, J. Howard Pew, and others, it was this: "The Bible is the infallible Word of God," and thus, "our only guide to living and working in this world."

A word here about "worldview" will help understand its use in this essay. David Naugle's

Worldview: The History of a Concept (GrandRapids: Eerdmans, 2002) shows how the concept has been used since the time of Immanuel Kant's *Critique of Judgment* (1790). Literally thousands of books and articles have been written on the subject. Moreover, since the 1890s, leading thinkers in America, such as William James, have used the term. Indeed, James was using it in the 1890s at the time Isaac Ketler was continuing his development of Grove City College and his own philosophical studies. Since the term "worldview" is a common element in the "rel/phil" program begun in President MacKenzie's first years at the College and continued in use ever since, it seems helpful to also use the term to describe Isaac Ketler's perspective, therein giving more continuity to this study's theme. "Biblical worldview" probably best describes the term's use here.

After studying the effects of Presbyterian theology on the lives of these people, marked by an exceptionally long period of spiritual leadership in the College, it seemed to me that the driving, yes, the animating influence of this theology constituted the very "soul of Grove City College." Today's College leaders continue to affirm and support this Pew/Ketler vision. Since the College is a human institution, the vision of its purpose has had its high points and low points. In other words, the spiritual life of the College did not flower, grow, and mature in a straight line from its founding to the present hour. This essay will, therefore, note changes and challenges in the development of its spiritual life.

Others have written about various aspects of Grove City College's history. David Dayton wrote about the educational development of the College; Hans Sennholz wrote about the College as an economic enterprise; and Lee Edwards expounded on the social history of the College as a chapter in America's rapidly growing collegiate movement in the twentieth century. In this context, the present study seeks to augment what Dayton, Sennholz, and Edwards have chronicled by emphasizing the spiritual core—the soul—of the College.

It will be helpful here to expand on the central theme in the development of the College's soul, noting a sub-theme that was often present. A central theme in the soul's development was the fact that it rested on the bedrock authority of the Bible which was, the founders believed, best summarized in the theology of the Westminster *Confession.* The sub-theme prominent in the College's early years was the murmur of pietism—a view of the Christian life which emphasized religious devotion and matters of religious experience— in American culture. It was always in tension with the Westminster Assembly's confessionalism, especially in frontier areas like Western Pennsylvania. An appreciation of this helps us understand vigorous student behavioral requirements evident from the first years of Ketler-sponsored educational institutions. The strictness of these requirements can only be appreciated as an expression of a latent pietism. By the second decade of the 20th century, Isaac Ketler's sturdy confessional theology migrated through decades of post-Westminster theology. That is to say, the larger Presbyterian Church was adjusting to what theologians call "Modernism," a view that does not begin with a total commitment to biblical authority but emphasizes instead human autonomy or the self-sufficiency of reason and scientific investigation. This challenge touched the College, too, a development J. Howard Pew saw clearly by the 1960s. Pew's answer was to hire Charles MacKenzie and charge him with the responsibility of returning the

College to the theological stance of its founders, i.e., a Biblically-based, Westminster-confessional worldview.

MacKenzie gathered people around him to help revitalize the spirit of this confessionalism. Significantly, advances had been made in the intellectual defense of Westminster theology during the previous decades in Reformed institutions, advances which included an emphasis on integrating faith and learning and the value of recognizing that all intellectual systems, or worldviews, rest on presuppositions. Mackenzie, though not previously a student of this development, encouraged and facilitated it. It was manifest in two important ways: One, in the creation of a core program which was anchored by a new introductory course called the Religion-Philosophy Keystone. A second significant aid in reviving the soul of the College initiated by MacKenzie was in his effort to "clean up student behavior," as J. Howard Pew put it. To the surprise of many, President MacKenzie found the right man for the job in the Religion/Philosophy Department. That man was the College's most popular teacher, philosophy professor, Ross Foster. MacKenzie appointed him as the new Dean of Students—a position that eventually evolved into Vice President for Student Affairs. The essence of Foster's contribution initially was in appointing self-confessing Christian students as Resident Advisors to incoming freshmen. These students soon initiated Bible Studies and other tools for spiritual development. Administrators and students from that era generally agree that self-consciously Christian students likely numbered only about 10 percent of the student body. Foster also urged MacKenzie to insist that a greater effort be placed on admitting more confessing Christian students in place of those who were, at best, nominal Christians. The effect of these changes was dramatic, but it took a long time to mature.

In sum, this essay assumes that the life of the soul of Grove City College passed through several stages. A first stage began when Isaac Ketler commenced his series of educational endeavors which resulted in the chartering of the College in November of 1884. As noted, Ketler developed a sturdy, Westminster-confessional worldview—with a hint of pietism lurking in the background. A second stage commenced in 1915, following the loss of three key leaders in five years. The life of the College's soul settled into a routine for the next 40 years. During this time a latent pietism surfaced. What the College's relationship with the emerging post-Westminster theology would be a continuing question. In this era the College also struggled with several other crucial issues. It was, for example, also plagued by fiscal and enrollment problems arising from the effects of WWI. Significantly, it achieved regional accreditation early in the 1920s only to lose it in 1955, due to weaknesses in curricular and administrative procedures. After 40 years this stage morphed into a third stage under the leadership of a new President, Stanley Harker. During his tenure there were many curricular reforms and accreditation was again regained. Student life took on a more expansive and robust flavor. Frat life and parties became more important, even dominating student social life.

Charles MacKenzie's appointment as President of the College in 1971 started a fourth, maturing stage in the life of the College's soul. When he retired in 1991, he had substantially achieved the two goals that Board Chairman J. Howard Pew had set for him at the time of his appointment. One of these was to clean up student life which had gained a "party school" reputation. As significant was the creation of a program that would again emphasize a Biblical basis for the school's intellectual life which occurred with the creation of a core program—the center of which was the religion/philosophy course. Known popularly as the "Religion Key" or "Rel-Phil," the two-semester-sequence Keystone 161-162 morphed into the Humanities courses which are now in place. It set the standard for the practice of integrating faith and learning. Jerry Combee followed Charles MacKenzie as the College's next President. Under his leadership the Keystone Curriculum was expanded to more than 30 hours. He injected a new level of rigor into the College's whole academic program as well. The academic curriculum which resulted from these changes was enhanced by the fact that Grove City College was the first college in the country to adopt the ambitious curriculum advocated by Lynn Cheney in the early 1990s.

    President Combee resigned in 1995 and was replaced a year later by economist John Moore. By that time the spiritual-based reforms begun by MacKenzie, reforms encompassing student behavior and curricular matters, had achieved their goal. The soul of the College had been reinvigorated and again enjoyed a healthy condition, as it had been in its founding stage. That being the case, the purpose of this essay, to give an account of the College's spiritual development, has been achieved. Further, since this has been an historical inquiry, tracing the subject much further chronologically would risk it becoming an exercise in journalism.

    At this writing, however, a new stage in the spiritual life of the College is unfolding. And why? The summer of 2014 saw the appointment of a new Grove City College President, the Hon. Paul McNulty '80. His goal is not only to tend to all of the College's needs generally, but to also focus on developing its intellectual life—a college's principal purpose—under the theme "faith and learning."

But, there is one more point to make in this prologue—a very personal one. This whole study is seen from my/our (my wife Kathryn has always been an integral part of this experience) perspective which is deeply affected by two experiences. First, I worked for J. Howard Pew as his personal research and writing assistant, living with my family on his estate. This experience gave me a profound understanding of J. Howard, both in his thinking and in the more mundane, though fascinating, aspects of his daily life—food, clothing, dwelling, good cigars, his plain personal car, and golf, but more on this later.

After my years living with Mr. Pew, and after his passing, I soon found myself in a second remarkable situation—teaching at "his college" as he liked to refer to it. The College's new President, Charles MacKenzie, invited me to stop at Grove City for an interview on my return to the University of Texas following a conference in Washington, D. C. I accepted and spent two days discussing his plans to revitalize the College's curriculum. His mission, he stated, was to deepen, enhance, and carry on the spiritual traditions of Grove City College—in this, continuing the College's maturation process. He thought I could help and offered me a contract. I accepted and moved to Grove City in the summer of 1972. Soon I was joined by many others, including Drs. Andrew Hoffecker and John Sparks. Ross Foster had joined the faculty two years earlier and was ready to help with President MacKenzie's revitalization plans. That was 42 years ago and I am still active as a Fellow for Humanities, Faith, and Culture in the Center for Vision & Values. Further, I have continuously studied many of the College's records, page by page, box-full by box-full for many summers.

I have been urged by some who know about my years living with J. Howard to include an account of it in this essay because it surely was a life-changing "Special Providence." And, I may be the last person standing who personally knew well this remarkable graduate of the class of 1900.

It seemed best, therefore, to begin this essay with an account of how I came to meet and work for J. Howard, living on his property and literally being in and out of his home. This is the basis of my personal view.

A last point here: That experience was the foundation of our understanding of the College's origins and maturation. It also gave us perspective on the spiritual mission of the College over the 42 years since we arrived in Grove City.

And more: This personal account of Grove City College's spiritual odyssey may be thought of as a "thank you" note to J. Howard Pew, a thank you for the life-long journey he set us on when he hired me to work for him more than 45 years ago. Looking back now, from the distance of a lifetime, it is remarkably clear and humbling to see how J. Howard's decision to hire me defined our lives as citizens in the Kingdom, a Kingdom in which he too was a citizen. A privilege indeed!

Chapter I
My Interest in the Soul of the College

Meeting J. Howard Pew: A Brief Overview

Yes, one of the great privileges of my life, one of the great blessings I have enjoyed, was the time spent working for J. Howard Pew during the last years of his life. Except for my father and my wife Kathryn, no one has had a greater impact on me than Mr. Pew. It was not just the impact of his power and money, though he was a very powerful and very wealthy man. Rather, it was the man himself, an exceedingly gracious and yet forceful personality, rare in any generation, and almost unknown in our time.

If we could ask J. Howard what he would want to be remembered for, I am sure that he would answer, though embarrassed by the question, "I would like to be remembered as a God-fearing Christian gentleman." Surely such a description is an accurate one. And, upon reflection, he would also add he would like to be remembered as a graduate of the Grove City College Class of '00 [1900], making that observation with a characteristic twinkle in his eye. J. Howard Pew was a person that many of us would do well to imitate, to use as a model for what we ought to be in both our public and personal lives. For this reason, I am pleased to present some observations and recollections of my years spent with him as part of this essay on the soul of Grove City College. These include not only how we met, what it was like working for him, but also a brief survey of some of his theological, political, and social views. And, it goes without saying that J. Howard was one of America's great 20th-century entrepreneurs. These characteristics were evident in our first meeting.

A. The Meeting

I met J. Howard Pew in a way that can only be described as Providential. While engaged in research in Grand Rapids, Michigan, a friend of mine told me about a phone call he received from a certain Mr. Pew of Philadelphia, seeking his service as a researcher and writer. My friend was involved with other commitments and could not pursue the matter. He suggested that I call Mr. Pew and discuss the possibility of my filling the position. I called.

After a half-hour conversation, he invited me to come and see him in Philadelphia. He asked if he could wire me some money to cover my expenses for the trip. I said no, as long as he reimbursed me following my trip. He agreed. After relating this conversation to my wife and summing up my plan to go to Philadelphia, she was skeptical—to put it mildly. Her prize observation was, "How do you know that he can afford to pay your expenses?" Her concern was based on the fact that we were living on modest savings as we finished a Ph.D. dissertation.

Four days later I was in Philadelphia ready to meet with Mr. Pew. I arrived at the Sun Oil Building fifteen minutes to nine. Passing guards, I took an elevator to the 19th floor and walked into a spacious reception area. Promptly at 9:00, his secretary of 40 years, Miss Baker, ushered me down a hallway and into a corner office where I met Mr. Pew. He rose from his chair behind a simple, though elegant, cherry table that he used as his desk, greeting me warmly in a deep voice. He was a large man, well over 6'2" tall and 200 pounds. His thick, bushy eye-brows, which moved when he talked, were a distinguishing feature of the man—also, no doubt, intimidating to most people.

Soon we were seated in leather easy chairs, spaced by a coffee table, beginning an uninterrupted four-hour talk. His first question was, "Are you an orthodox Christian?" To him this meant, "Are you in the Reformed tradition theologically?" I answered, "Yes," and then outlined how I had grown up in the Dutch Reformed Church.

Obviously pleased with my answer, he began a soliloquy about how he had for many years employed someone to work for him personally on matters relating to church history and theological issues. He was especially interested, he said, in continuing his support of research and writing on the life of John Calvin, the documents of the Westminster Assembly, and the American Revolution.

For several hours he told about the various research projects he had supported, including the ground-breaking work of the distinguished historian of the Reformation, Robert M. Kingdon. With Pew's support, Kingdon had microfilmed the records of Geneva's Company of Pastors in the time of Calvin. Parts of this work subsequently appeared as books and articles. He also supported scholars working on the documents of the Westminster Assembly, which was the theological foundation of his beloved Presbyterian Church. He also underwrote numerous studies relating to the founders of the American Revolution.

Needless to say, I was impressed with the grasp that he had as a layman of these subjects, subjects that I myself had worked on for many years. Finally, sometime after 1:00, he asked if I would be interested in having a sandwich with him. With what energy I could muster—I am one of those who prefers an early lunch—I agreed that a sandwich would be a good idea. Without a word he rose from his chair, went to a closet and took out a heavy overcoat—it was January—and walked from the room. I offered to help him with the coat, but his reply was, "Thank you, I don't need any help." Down the hall, down the elevator, through the garage, across a street and into an imposing building we walked—it was the Philadelphia Racket Club.

Without saying a word, he strode to a desk and scribbled a note which he handed to a waiter. Thereafter we were seated and served our lunch. The sandwich turned out to be a slice of prime rib served on a piece of toast. Some sandwich!

Over lunch we struck a bargain. I would work for him researching and writing in the areas mentioned, and I would help him with speeches and troublesome correspondence dealing with theological matters. I also reviewed manuscripts by writers seeking his support for publication.

After our return to his office, he arranged for me to go to New York the next day to visit with some friends of his who were about to begin publishing the *Presbyterian Layman*—a newspaper which probed contemporary events and movements within the PCUSA denomination which were of interest to traditional Presbyterians within the denomination. He asked that I help them editorially for the next few months. I then spoke with Jim Cochran, the publisher, and he gave me instructions as to how to get to his New York office the next day. I left J. Howard after we settled on a time when I would again meet him after his six-week cruise. I called my wife on a land-line phone (no cell phones in those days) with a poor connection. I told her that I was going to New York before I returned home the next evening. Later, she reported that she wondered all day, "What in the world was I doing in New York!"

I arrived the next day at the offices of the *Layman*

at 9:00. After becoming acquainted with the *Layman* project, we spent the lunch hour with part of the staff and a number of New York publication specialists—mapping out the forthcoming first edition of the paper. Soon it was 3:00 and time for me to leave if I were to catch my flight back to Michigan. Jim Cochran excused himself for a few minutes and then returned and said to me, "You can stay longer; I arranged for you to make that flight."

Two hours later, our meeting ended and he told me that a car was waiting for me at the entrance to the building, that it would take me to the foot of Wall Street where a helicopter would take me to the Newark Airport to meet my plane. This was a remarkable experience for a young academic from the Midwest! I pondered the way "big-time" business people solved problems as my flight headed west. Thereafter I commuted by air from Michigan to New York City and the offices of the *Layman* each Thursday morning, returning each evening, for the next six weeks.

B. A First Visit to Knollwood—the Pew Estate

By that time, J. Howard had returned from his Mediterranean cruise and called to see when I could come to his home for a weekend visit. The following Friday was the date and he told me that his driver, Walter, would be in front of the airport terminal in a black car with a white top when I arrived. Upon arriving, I left the terminal and there was Walter, a tall, distinguished-looking African-American with a bright smile.

Walter assumed that I would ride in the back seat of the limo, but I asked if it would be all right if I rode up front with him. With his characteristic smile, he agreed and off we went. Soon we were at the front door of Knollwood, as the Pew home was called.

Once in the house, I was welcomed by Mr. Pew's housekeeper Sheila, an Irish "ball of fire," standing perhaps five feet tall and maybe 100 pounds on the scale and about 70 years old. She ushered me up to the second floor while insisting that Walter carry my bag. Down a long hall we went to a room at the end. "You can stay in here," she said—no, ordered me! Continuing, "This is where Mr. Nixon and Mr. Graham stay when they come here." It was clear that she was delighted to help me with anything I might need or want while there. Dinner would be at 7:00.

I came down a bit before 7:00 and met Mr. Pew in his sun porch on the south side of the house. He greeted me warmly as always, and then we went into the 60-foot-long dining room and seated ourselves at one end of a very long table. That was the first of many dinners that Kathryn and I would have there. We visited that evening and much of the next day. Sunday breakfast was at 9:00, served on a small oval table at one end of the dining room. Following, we sat on the porch and read the news for a time and then Sheila appeared and announced that it was time for church, handing Mr. Pew twenty dollars for collection. He looked at his large pocket watch—as he often did. Soon we were near the front door where he put on an old raincoat and hat and stepped out. I expected to see Walter and "the car" there, but to my surprise a 5-year-old deep green Oldsmobile, in mint condition, awaited us. J. Howard sat behind the wheel and off we whizzed, down the winding drive to Old Gulf Road, then west for one mile to Montgomery Avenue where Ardmore Presbyterian Church was situated on the corner. That speedy (to say the least) ride took not much more than a minute, it seemed to me! He parked across the street, we crossed, and entered the front door of the Church, moved up the near-aisle about six rows, where he paused, took off his battered coat and hat, dropping them at his feet as he entered the pew. Within a minute, the preacher mounted the platform and the service began. Time being valuable, not a moment was wasted in any area of his life.

When the service was over, we retraced our steps, with a nod now and again to fellow parishioners, thereafter driving back down Old Mill Creek Road. We had lunch and some conversation after which he bid me good-bye. We had plans for me to return shortly with my wife and look at a house on the property that he thought we should live in. Later, Walter drove me to the airport and in a few hours I was again home in Grand Rapids, pondering with my wife the extraordinary events of the past few weeks.

C. Moving to Knollwood

A few weeks later, my wife Kathryn and I flew to Philadelphia, and were picked up by Walter and deposited at the front door of the Pew house, where bubbling Sheila greeted us with open arms. She and Kathryn were instant friends. We were ushered to the same room on the second floor I had used a few weeks earlier. At dinner we joined J. Howard for a roast beef feast. He gave Kathryn a portable button, which buzzed in the kitchen, with instructions about using it to call for service. He gave me the job of slicing the roast. As Sheila served from the platter, J. Howard had difficulty maneuvering a slice onto his plate. In exasperation, and with a typical twinkle in his eyes, and a glance at Kathryn, he set his fork down and placed the meat on his plate with his fingers! Obviously J. Howard was a practical man, too.

The next day was a memorable and remarkable one, also. He had arranged for one of his groundskeepers to take us to another of three large houses on his 57-acre estate. We entered and looked through the 17 rooms—seven of which were quarters for cooking and cleaning help. One living room alone was at least 50 feet long with doors opening onto a veranda that ran along two sides of the house—like MAP dormitory on the Grove City College campus. There were few furnishings in the house and its size was overwhelming.

At dinner that evening Mr. Pew asked us what we thought of the house. Reluctantly, we noted that it had few furnishings and was very large. As to the furnishings, he said, "We can furnish it." He sensed that the size was a problem and said that he had another idea. As it turned out the next day, he sent word that we should go to the "cottage," a modest three-bedroom dwelling near the back of the property and introduce ourselves to his grandson Victor and his wife Lisa. They would soon be moving out to a new house that they were building.

We visited the cottage—about seven rooms—and decided that it would be just right for us once it was vacant. Within weeks we moved and settled in the cottage and arranged for some repairs and decorating at Mr. Pew's request. J. Howard had also seen to it that I had a study in a nearby carriage house he had remodeled. He provided for our needs and more. These included such items as a copy machine, travel expenses for research, utilities, health insurance, books, and a generous salary.

Over the next years we lived and worked at Knollwood. We were really part of the household, befriended by Sheila and others working there, including

Walter. Regularly we had dinner and conversations with Mr. Pew. And, he and I would have "business" meetings from time to time in his study in the house.

It was while living and working at Knollwood that I gained insight into J. Howard Pew's thinking and basic ideas. We turn now to a brief survey of some of them.

D. Religious views of J. Howard Pew

J. Howard Pew was above all a professing Biblical Christian. The most moving experience of his life, he said, was the occasion when he was ordained as a Ruling Elder in the Ardmore Presbyterian Church. He was not, however, merely a Presbyterian. He was an educated devotee of the historic theology which can be traced back through the Westminster Assembly to the teachings of John Calvin. He was convinced that most of the theological difficulties encountered by the Presbyterian Church could be traced to the fact that it had strayed from this theology. One of his prized possessions was a 1611(original) edition of the *King James Bible*. As a serious Bible student, he parked this boxed volume next to his chair in the main floor's reading room. We perused it from time to time, too.

The theology of Calvin was best expressed, he thought, in the writings of the Westminster Assembly of Divines. He was a strong supporter of the Westminster Assembly's *Confession of Faith,* having read it dozens of times. He knew much about the lives and other writings of the men who wrote it. The Assembly's *Confession* was "the finest theological document ever written," he would frequently say.

What especially attracted J. Howard Pew to the *Confession* was its unequivocal defense of liberty in the name of biblical authority. It stated that "God alone is Lord of the conscience and has set it free from the doctrines and commandments of men." From this he derived his most characteristic statement about religion and society, namely, that "from Christian freedom come all of our other freedoms." Political freedom and economic freedom were the result of religious freedom, that is, freedom of conscience to worship God as one saw fit.

In his view, the Constitution of the United States was the best expression of the political freedoms that flowed from religious freedom. In addition, the free market order was the best economic outgrowth of freedom that flowed from Christian liberty. Religion was healthier, politics were more vital, and economic systems were more productive when men possessed freedom of conscience, that is, Christian freedom.

Believing that from Christian freedom come all of the other freedoms, J. Howard Pew vigorously supported those people and causes that defended freedom in religion, politics, and economics. And, he chastised those who were opposed to freedom in these realms. He opposed socialism because it undermined political and economic freedom. He opposed those in the Presbyterian Church who concentrated power in the hands of a few clerical leaders.

In defense of Christian freedom, J. Howard supported a large number of causes. For example, he founded the *Presbyterian Layman* as a means to call Presbyterians back to a biblical view of the Church and its duties. He thought that the first task of the Church was to preach the Gospel at home and abroad. When the Church involved itself in social issues beyond traditional acts of charity, he felt it suffered and was diverted from its first calling—preaching the Gospel.

He was among the first to recognize the preaching talents of Billy Graham in 1948. From that day to his death, he was Graham's principal supporter. Graham was a frequent guest at Pew's home. With Graham, Nelson Bell, and Carl F.H. Henry he founded *Christianity Today* as a magazine dedicated to expounding the virtues of biblical theology.

J. Howard Pew was not content to merely support others who spoke of the value of Christian freedom and biblical theology. He traveled and spoke fearlessly—yes, fearlessly—about these matters himself. One of the remarkable experiences I had while working for him was to accompany him on some of these speaking tours. Picture, if you can, a man in his mid-to-late 80s, getting up in front of large audiences and speaking to them, <u>without a note</u>, on basic matters such as the separation of church and state. It took vision. It took courage. It took dedication and energy. He traveled to dozens and dozens of cities all over the nation to present his views on Christian freedom. On one such trip, for example, he spoke in Seattle, Portland, San Francisco, Los Angeles, Denver, and Dallas in five days. This by a man who was 88 years old! What a model for a young man—myself—to emulate! And, the consistency, clarity, and constancy of the message never wavered.

E. Social Views of J. Howard Pew

Christianity was more than theology to J. Howard. It was also a matter of practice. As a Christian, blessed with great wealth, he had social duties as well. He was very conscious of this fact. The first principle of the Christian life, after preaching the Gospel, was charity. Charity, for him, began at home. In the years I lived with J. Howard, I witnessed many charitable acts and heard about dozens more. It would take a large book to recount them. A few examples may suggest something of the range of his generosity and stewardship.

One of the gardeners who worked on the Pew estate had medical problems in his family which cost a great deal of money. Hearing about this, Mr. Pew called Harry in and inquired about the details. Immediately, he paid all his bills, unpaid by insurance, with a personal check. Pew also had a word of advice for Harry. "Don't pay the doctor all at once," he advised. "Pay him a little at a time. It helps to keep his bill lower next time." Others on the grounds testified to similar acts of charity, including covering the full cost of a college education at Grove City College, of course, for the children of his household and grounds-keeping help.

Members of the family—not all of them were wealthy—related to me situations in which J. Howard also helped them with unexpected medical bills. A story circulated around the Sun Oil Company about an injured worker who spent weeks in the hospital. J. Howard paid all expenses and also visited the man every day for weeks on his way home from the office.

Philadelphia hospitals, medical schools, orphanages, and other helping agencies received his aid for decades. The Boy Scouts, George Junior Republic, a "troubled youth" institution in Grove City, and dozens of similar agencies also received his help. The new building for the Presbyterian Historical Society was made possible because of a generous gift from J. Howard Pew. He did not, however, like publicity about the gifts he gave. A certain hospital was burned out years ago and came to Pew for funds. He gave them $250,000 and asked not to be named. After the hospital released information to the press about his gift, they never again received a donation.

There was one institution, however, that was closer to J. Howard Pew's heart than all the others. It was Grove City College. He gave more money to it than to any other institution. Though he was of the Class of '00, his motivation for generosity to the College was based upon his belief that education was the key to success. He supported this school because he believed that it was important for people of <u>ordinary means</u> to have an opportunity <u>at a reasonable cost</u> for a good education <u>from a Christian perspective</u>.

Several times a year he made trips to the school to speak and review its operation. Every week he was on the phone to the President to help out in any way that he could. He had a vision for this school: to teach the value of freedom and the virtue of Christian ethics. Even in his last months he spoke of these matters while on the campus. The last significant act of his long life was an effort to persuade Charles MacKenzie to accept the offer to become the next President of the College. He was sure that MacKenzie was the man to revive and carry on the vision that he and the founders had for the school. J. Howard would be proud, no doubt, to see that much has been done to assure that the value of freedom and the virtue of Christian ethics have been integrated into the core of the College's curriculum.

J. Howard Pew was a conscientious steward of his wealth. He spent little money on himself. He enjoyed a good Havana cigar—about three a day; he appreciated plain but tasty food—no tea or coffee or vanilla; instead, orange juice, milk, chocolate and an occasional bed-time glass of Harvey's Bristol Cream; and, he drove a functional automobile, that is, a 5-year-old Oldsmobile. His only play—besides bridge with his sisters—was a game of golf twice a week. Beyond that, his needs were modest. His clothing was hand-tailored in New York but worn for years and years, frequently until threadbare. Miss Sheila scolded him on occasion for this.

It is interesting to observe that Mr. Pew did not consider himself a wealthy man, a point he made from time to time. What he meant, of course, was that most of the wealth he controlled either directly or indirectly, was tied up in capital investment—in the plant and equipment of the Sun Oil Company [Sunoco]. From the records available, it would seem that he had access at any one time to some 25 million dollars, not a large amount for one who had built a firm worth several billions at the time.

Each year he used a little of this money for his household and personal needs and gave away the rest, either as cash or in Sun Oil stock. He enjoyed giving away his money to causes that he thought just and useful. Charity for him began at home, in his community, and in supporting "his" college.

In mealtime prayers, and in evening prayers, usually spoken aloud at about 6:30 before dinner, he frequently sought strength and the ability to help "make the world a finer place in which to live." In other words, he prayed for the spiritual strength to be a good steward of his time, talent, and money.

F. Political Views of J. Howard Pew

Christian freedom meant more than mere personal freedom to J. Howard Pew. Christian freedom, freedom of conscience, was a first principle of the political order as well. Political freedom meant for him limited government. The Founding Fathers of the American Revolution stated the principles of political liberty in the Constitution, a document unequaled among the political writings of the world, Pew believed.

He, like his close personal friend Herbert Hoover, believed that the New Deal philosophy of government as the primary agency of social welfare was a direct challenge to the principles of freedom. It was during the era of the New Deal that he began to speak out against "the evils of big government," as he called it. From that time until his death he actively opposed what he termed the "creeping socialism" of the New Deal mentality. At the same time, he actively supported those people and institutions that stood for limited government.

J. Howard himself was never active in party politics, though he supported the Republican Party. His brother, Joseph Newton Pew, Jr., was the family's front man in party politics. He did, however, support selected candidates in Pennsylvania and at the national level. He met Richard Nixon in the late 1940s through Billy Graham and supported him for many years. Near the end of J. Howard's life, Nixon was elected President. Pew took personal satisfaction in this because he had supported Nixon since he was introduced to him in 1948. I recall being present when Mr. Pew received a birthday gift from President Nixon in 1969. He was especially pleased and honored by the hand-written note from the President. The present was a portrait of Nixon surrounded with postage stamps which bore the pictures of Presidents. Several times that year he was an overnight guest at the White House. It must have taken him back many years to the time when he was President Hoover's guest.

Fortunately, J. Howard Pew died before Watergate began to unfold. I am sure that Pew, man of principle that he was, would have found Watergate agonizing and too much to believe about a man whom he had known and trusted for several decades, a man whom he had as a guest in his home many times.

G. Final Thoughts About J. Howard Pew

As I reflect upon J. Howard Pew, several of his basic personal qualities come to mind. He was, first, a man of uncommon integrity. His word was his bond. When he said "yes," he meant yes. He did not straddle the fence. He did not equivocate. Many times in his business career he refused to do business with people if he was convinced that they were not honest. He expected simple honesty from others just as he practiced it himself.

Implied in what has been said already is a second characteristic, namely, that he was a conscientious steward of his time, talent, and money. He planned every minute of the day by his big pocket watch, yet he was not driven by it. He wasted few words. When talking about a subject, he would likely pause for a time—what seemed like minutes to his listeners—and then deliver a brief, cogent statement on the subject.

J. Howard Pew was, thirdly, a man of uncommon ability, even brilliant. This was a fact evident to all who knew him. Late in his long life he could master a difficult subject. For example, when his wife was sick with what the medical people called an incurable blood disease, he studied medical books and mastered the basics of blood chemistry. In time, he hired people to research her problem, sparing no expense, and with knowledge and understanding, he oversaw the project. In due course, they came up with a cure. As a result, she lived another 13 years. His ability and drive were also evident in his playing of bridge, studying theology, making business deals, and in many other ways.

Fourth, Mr. Pew was also a man of vision, a quality found in all great business leaders. He saw the future needs of the oil business long before others. For example, he pushed in the early 1960s for the building of a plant in Canada which could extract oil from the tar sands of Alberta. Over the objections of many of his associates, the plant was built. Today it is a profitable operation for Sun Company. He saw that personal liberty was being eroded by a growing government long before most others. He understood the value of education for ordinary people at a time when education was still the privilege of a few. He early grasped the necessity of sounding the alarm to his fellow Presbyterians about the dangers of straying from biblical principles.

Fifth, J. Howard Pew was a very human person, though his shyness obscured this dimension of his personality to some. I recall how he came to our dwelling on his estate several times to speak with my wife. He wanted to get her reaction to remarks he was to make to a women's group in the local church.

He lingered a while to chat with our sons who played at his feet while he spoke. And, at Halloween, he enjoyed having the boys come to his house dressed in costumes. He laughed heartily as they attempted to scare him with their masked faces. And, then there was the time at the conclusion of a dinner when a guest asked permission to smoke a cigarette. Direct man that he was, he objected. Then he began a long and lucid lecture on the chemistry of smoke and how the benzene qualities of the paper could cause cancer—this in 1970, long before modern cancer research. The guest was offered a cigar instead. This incident testifies to his training as a chemical engineer at Grove City and at Boston Tech, as he liked to refer to MIT before it was MIT. It also testifies to his remarkably inquisitive nature, still so in his 87th year.

Finally, J. Howard Pew was concerned about civilization itself, especially about the future of

American civilization. Few active business leaders think on this scale, but he did. He was determined to use his money to help assure that the American society of the future would be better, that is, "more free and more prosperous," than it had been when he began his career. For him, this meant fighting for the principles of Christian freedom, for, as he said so often, "from Christian freedom flow all of our other freedoms."

H. Saying Good-bye

And then came the last time we saw him. He was very ill in the summer of 1971. He knew the end was near. We agreed that it soon would be time for me to return to college teaching. Weeks later, when we had packed up the moving van and prepared to leave, we stopped in the courtyard of his home. I went in to say goodbye. We talked a while. Then he asked about my wife and three young sons. Learning they were outside, he rose with difficulty from his chair and came outside, bidding them farewell, one by one as they stood by the car. We watched as he walked, slowly now, back into the house.

In a few months, while attending a meeting with Billy Graham—whom I had met through J. Howard, subsequently writing some speeches for him—word came that J. Howard had died. I flew back to Philadelphia with Rev. Graham to attend the funeral. I again spent a few hours at Knollwood in Ardmore. As I left, I turned and looked again at the courtyard, and at the huge front door, where I had last seen him. I thought to myself, "Freedom has lost a great friend!" Walking away, I knew that the world was a better place in which to live because J. Howard Pew had been here, 89 years and 10 months.

Chapter 2
The Source of the College's Soul

Western Pennsylvania was settled and populated in the 19th century by large numbers of God-fearing Christians and a large percentage of them were Presbyterians. The soul of Grove City College, that animating spiritual force that defines the College's purpose and mission, was a child of these Presbyterians in general, and of several Pews and Ketlers in particular. While the soul became evident in the last quarter of the 19th century as the College was conceived, gestated, and born, its spiritual quality is best understood through a look at the Pew clan decades before. Isaac Ketler's spiritual contributions emerged later after the College was born, a topic we shall cover following an account of the early Pews.

A. The Pew Family

The record is clear that the Pews, staunch Presbyterians, came to America from England during the English Civil War/Puritan Revolution of the 1640s, settling in Virginia. By the time of the American Revolution a number of them moved to the Western Pennsylvania frontier. Over the next decades some stayed in the fledgling town of Pittsburgh while John Pew, born in 1769, traveled north sixty miles to Mercer County in 1797. There we pick up the story of the Grove City College Pews.

John's son, John Hancock Pew was born in Mercer County in 1800 and married Nancy Glenn in 1824. Of their 10 children only five survived to adulthood, one of which was Joseph Newton Pew, one of the College's founders. Joseph Newton was born in 1848 and died in 1910. Before turning to an account of his career, the spiritual and moral qualities of the Pew family deserve consideration because they characterized Joseph Newton and his son J. Howard as they figured prominently in the founding and development of the College.

Further, as the Pew clan grew and developed during the 19th century, a signal characteristic of American denominations was their tendency to split apart and form new congregations, even among rock-ribbed Presbyterians. Sometimes these splits were for practical reasons, for example the desire of one part of a congregation to move West with the frontier. On the other hand, congregations often split over social and political issues, or on theological ones. At the time of the Civil War, Presbyterians split—largely between the North and the South—on the question of slavery. Moreover, in the 19th century there were numerous revivals, especially on the frontier. One issue that was prominent in these revivals was a tension between the place of piety in the Christian life on the one hand and a solid confessional theology on the other. As Presbyterians, the Pews were definitely on the side of confessional theology, the Westminster Assembly's Confession and catechisms. Pietism, however, lurked in the back benches of Presbyterian congregations as well.

A note on pietism here will be useful. One of the themes in Church History has been an ebb and flow between emphasis on intellectual elements of Christian faith and an emphasis on personal experience, a need to separate from the world, and living a life that focuses on an inner life of holiness. The term *pietism* was probably first used to describe a movement in German Lutheran churches in the 17th century. Brethren and Methodist churches are, to a large degree, an outgrowth of this movement. To the extent that persons or churches are defined by pietism, they are less likely to focus on formal theology. In a broad perspective, every Christian ought to have a good balance between an organized understanding of Biblical teachings (theology) and a deep personal, devotional-based piety. The Reformers, Luther and Calvin, themselves modeled such a balance. The point here is that a tension between these elements of the Christian life continued through the 19th century and may be seen in the culture of Western Pennsylvania into the middle of the 20th century. Indeed, it was a factor as the College emerged and grew.

Another observation or two on this point will be helpful here. Church historian W. Andrew Hoffecker suggests that the Westminster Assembly's theology is the best summary of Reformed principles. This perspective was, of course, the backbone of Presbyterianism from its inception in the 1640s down to the middle of the 20th century when it was challenged by rationalistic Modernism. That is to say, traditional Presbyterianism was based on the belief that the Bible was the authoritative Word of God, and thus, the basis of a Christian life. Most recent forms of Presbyterianism have assumed that reason and cultural experience are normative for theology and life—a much different view. Lest there be any confusion, we emphasize here that the Pews stood four-square on the traditional view of the Bible as the only authority for faith and life. Piety was, of course, present in their lives as well, though in a secondary way.

The 19th-century Pews were principled people in a practical way also. For example, in pre-Civil-War Mercer, PA a dispute erupted about whether the Presbyterian congregation should support slavery. The majority concluded that it should. Elder John Hancock

Pew, Joseph Newton's father, however, argued that slavery was immoral; leaving that church, he began, along with others, the Free Presbyterian Church. But, he did more. With the rest of his family, he aided the "under-ground railroad"—the network of people in the North who passed along slaves trying to make their way to the Canadian border and freedom. This sense of fairness and moral rectitude echoed down through the next generations of Pews as well.

In addition, the Pews were mission-minded. While most Native Americans who had lived in the region for a long time moved or were driven further West by 1800, some continued wandering about Western Pennsylvania, peacefully most often. From time to time a few Native Americans were befriended by John H. and Nancy Glenn Pew. Nancy was known for teaching Native Americans a number of civilizing domestic chores, including sewing, certain kinds of cooking, and more. We can be sure that in the process, the Pews told the Native Americans about the Gospel. Whether many Native Americans became Presbyterians, we do not know.

The Mercer County Pews like most Presbyterians worshiped in their home each morning and in Church twice on Sunday. The children were catechized either weekly in church or at home. A catechism is, of course, a summary of Christian doctrine in a question-and-answer format. Martin Luther (1483-1546) popularized the catechetical idea as a way to teach young people. John Calvin (1509-1564) followed Luther's lead and composed his own catechism. His catechism, in turn, was a model for the Scottish Reformed Church, and also a model for the Westminster *Shorter Catechism* of the 1640s. Editions of this document were published many times in America, especially after the Revolution.

Western Pennsylvania Presbyterians, including the Pews, used the *Shorter Catechism* to teach their children. This practice remained into the 20th century until catechizing ceased as a means of theological instruction.

Obviously, catechizing, along with sermons based on the Westminster Confession, provided all the Pews—male and female alike—with a solid biblical theology. And more. It provided them with moral principles for daily life for which they had a solid reputation.

While many Mercer County Pews were very accomplished, two stand out as titans in the business world and in the founding and development of Grove City College: Joseph Newton and his son J. Howard. Joseph Newton was born in 1848, while his son J. Howard was born in 1882. Leaving J. Howard for the moment, we turn to a consideration of J. N.'s remarkable accomplishments, both as an entrepreneur and as benefactor of the College.

B. **The Significance of Joseph Newton Pew**

1. In General

It goes without saying that he was an Elder in whatever congregation he happened to be a member, whether in Bradford, in Pittsburgh's Liberty Street Presbyterian congregation, or later in Bryn Mawr. And, as always, he championed the Westminster tradition of theology.

After an extensive review and re-review of the records of the founding of the College and the development of Sun Oil, one can conclude only one thing regarding Joseph Newton Pew: He was the **towering** figure in the development of both. And, one may be certain that the College would likely have failed, or never developed beyond being a small academy or normal school by 1900 if Joseph Newton Pew had not joined forces with Isaac Ketler. That is to say, that it did succeed was the result of J. N.'s great success in the oil business and his decision to financially help his former student Isaac Ketler develop the College in the mid-1890s.

His help was two-fold—well, three-fold. First, he used his own great wealth to support the College, and he persuaded other Pittsburgh business magnets to contribute money to the College as well, not the least of which was his friend Andrew Carnegie. Second, by 1894 he joined the College's Board and urged a reorganization of the school's Charter, changing it from a stock company to a charitable institution, therein making it more attractive to contributors. Third, J. N. assumed the chairmanship of the College's Board of Trustees and provided steady guidance to the less experienced Isaac Ketler. In this capacity he encouraged the continued development of the College's spiritual life, easy enough to do, no doubt, while working with fellow Presbyterian stalwart, Isaac Ketler.

2. Joseph Newton Pew: Entrepreneur

The success of the College has depended on the wealth of the Pew family, but most people associated with the College have no idea how the Pew wealth was created. We sum up that story by focusing on how it was initially generated through the vision and genius of Joseph Newton Pew. After his death in 1912, his son J. Howard followed in his footsteps, continuing to guide Sun Company and the College until his own death in 1971.

Joseph Newton Pew (1848-1912), born in Mercer County, attended private schools, sometimes called "select schools," which were parent-owned and operated, and staffed by a minister or would-be preacher, later attending Mercer Academy also. A very accomplished student, he was asked to teach in a one-room school in nearby London, staying 1866-1869. Having saved some money, he went on to attend Edinboro Normal School for one year, Edinboro being the first normal school in Western Pennsylvania.

But business beckoned, likely influenced by the fact that his father sold real estate as a side-line to his farming. Pew moved to Titusville, which was booming due the discovery of oil there. He sold and traded land and oil leases. Next, he recognized that natural gas, an oil-pumping by-product, would be valuable as fuel for street lights and domestic use. He then established a firm to pipe natural gas to Bradford. With a partner, he also piped gas to nearby Olean, New York.

A few years later, he brought the same system to Pittsburgh, commuting back and forth from Bradford for several years, eventually moving from "frontier-town" Bradford to Pittsburgh. Meanwhile, he invented a pump which maintained a constant pressure for the gas in the city's pipelines. Then he created and sold several gas pipeline systems, including The Peoples Natural Gas Company, which still serves the city of Pittsburgh. Pew also used his inventive skills to create a gas meter to measure the flow of gas to customers.

An interesting historical footnote about Joseph Newton Pew in his early Pittsburgh years is the fact that he offered to supply Andrew Carnegie's steel plant with natural gas for **free**. He did so because the gas supply was gigantic and still viewed as a by-product of oil-pumping. Carnegie was so enthused that he agreed, but insisted that he pay Pew for the gas!

Inventor and visionary that he was, qualities that also characterized his son J. Howard, Joseph Newton Pew could see that there was an even greater future in the oil business itself. After the discovery of large oil fields in Ohio and Texas by 1900, he sold his gas businesses and focused on oil. Later with this in mind, no doubt, J. Howard liked to quote his father who said, "Put all of your eggs in one basket and hang on to the basket." Pew soon built a refinery in Toledo to process the flow of oil out of central Ohio. Next, he built a refinery in Marcus Hook, PA to process oil brought from Texas. These new ventures now used the name Sun Oil. A Pew ground-breaking development was the creation of a series of oil tankers used to transport oil from Texas to Marcus Hook. This system allowed Sun Company to avoid the use of railroads which were virtual monopolies controlled by the Rockefellers of Standard Oil fame. In addition, along with many subsidiary firms, Sun Oil developed over 100 oil-based products by the first years of the 20th century. Soon Philadelphia became the home of Sun Oil, and in 1904 the Pew Family moved there too, the next year purchasing a substantial home in Bryn Mawr.

By 1900, Joseph Newton Pew had accumulated great wealth, yet never forsaking his strong faith and always desiring to support Kingdom ventures. Since his ties to Grove City College had been well-established early in the previous decade, it is not surprising that it had become his favorite eleemosynary institution. Thus, the link between Pew wealth and a firm, biblically-based faith, initiated by Joseph Newton Pew and Grove City College was complete.

C. Isaac Ketler: 1853-1910

We turn now to a sketch of Isaac Ketler's educational innovations once he arrived in Pine Grove. This, of course, includes the time when he sought out his former teacher Joseph Newton Pew for support of his educational endeavors.

Gathering data about the early stages of Isaac Ketler's life is problematic, at least that is the case when it comes to generally available published information. Further research in archives, court records, and similar data might provide more detail about Isaac Ketler's early life. Existing information has some inconsistencies in it. One involves evidence of how and where he lived before he arrived at the age of 23 in Pine Grove (later known as Grove City) in 1876. Moreover, data about his education once he arrived in Pine Grove is confusing as well, especially on the question of when and how long he studied at the numerous institutions that appear in accounts of his life. Published accounts, for example, which comment on when and how long Ketler studied in Edinboro Normal School simply do not agree. And, references to his studies in Lebanon, Ohio, have different names for the school he attended and different dates as to when he was there.

Despite these inconsistencies, we can bring some order to the facts of Ketler's early years, down to the time he arrived in Pine Grove, and, an account of his studies will show that his educational achievements were considerable, most of them occurring after he arrived in Pine Grove. A full account of Ketler's achievements must include his remarkable spiritual life which encompasses three dimensions: his studies (especially theological subjects); his religious emphasis as an educational leader; and his preparation and writing of his remarkable book *The Pilgrims* in 1910 (the Introduction is included as Appendix D).

1. Early Years and Education

Isaac Conrad Ketler was born in central Pennsylvania's Northumberland County in 1853, one of twelve children born to Adam and Mary Ketler. When Isaac was 4 years old, the family moved to Blacktown in Western Pennsylvania's Mercer County. We do know that the Ketlers were farmers and also had a produce business. Like most of their neighbors the Ketlers were devout Presbyterians, typically worshiping daily at home and in church on Sunday. Isaac probably attended a select school. We know for certain that he attended school in nearby London, likely at about age 13. His teacher in London was none other than 18-year-old Joseph Newton Pew, the same Pew who joined him later in developing the College. Pew taught in London from 1866 to 1869.

Isaac left home at age 17 to seek further education against the wishes of his father. It is at this point that the sequence of when and where Ketler studied is vague. It may also be true that he worked in a logging camp and a brick factory to make money to pay for his studies.

What he did between 1870/71 and 1876 when he arrived in Pine Grove includes the following events, though the sequence is uncertain. Some writers state that he attended a school known as the National Army School in Lebanon, Ohio, before 1875. Another reference to Ketler's Lebanon education suggests he attended the National Normal School there. The latter is probably a correct reference because Isaac Ketler is listed as a prominent graduate in this two-year institution's records, now housed in the Warren County

(Ohio) Historical Society. Old Pine Grove records also indicate that he came to Pine Grove from that institution when he was hired to teach in Pine Grove's select (private elementary or grammar) school in 1876.

On the other hand, records of Venango County, east of Pine Grove, indicate that Scrubgrass Presbyterian Church had a new academy in 1875 and that 22-year-old Isaac Ketler was this academy's first principal—academy at the time was another name for a private elementary school. In his *Mid the Pines* (1971), David Dayton states that Ketler also attended Edinboro Normal School and was graduated from there in 1875. He also notes that Ketler taught school in New Hamburg and then in Emlenton, probably referring to the Scrubgrass Academy mentioned in the Venango County records cited above.

A look at the purpose of normal schools gives us perspective on Ketler's early education. Normal schools were a 19th-century creation aimed at taking graduates of the eighth grade (select school/elementary) through a two-year program which would train them to be teachers. Thus, graduates of a normal school's two year program, including Isaac Ketler, had at least part of what we now call high school training. Some normal schools offered more courses than others. Thus, while at National Normal School, Ketler was able to study Greek and Latin. Since the normal school program is for two years, it does not appear that Ketler had earned a bachelor's degree by the time he arrived in Pine Grove in1876. It's possible that he did that by correspondence courses through National Normal School during his first years in Pine Grove.

From some sketchy records, however, we might infer that he finished his bachelor degree studies at Allegheny College. He may have transferred credits from his time at the National Normal School in Ohio to Allegheny College to satisfy bachelor degree requirements. Consider further, that it was common practice at that time for schools to offer a master's degree to students without further study, three years after they had finished a bachelor's degree without even having set foot on the campus to get this degree. Isaac Ketler was, indeed, awarded a master's degree from Allegheny College in 1882.

Ketler did additional graduate study beyond studies at Allegheny College after his arrival in Pine Grove. He was awarded a Ph.D. from Wooster University in 1884. At that time one could obtain a Ph.D. through correspondence courses, a practice Grove City College followed once it obtained its Charter in 1884. That is to say, Ketler never went to Wooster, Ohio, to study. He did write an essay for the Wooster faculty that was presented for the degree.

A few years later, Ketler pursued another degree by enrolling in Western Theological Seminary on the north side of Pittsburgh, attending sessions while on leave from the College. Noteworthy here is the fact that while attending Western Seminary, Ketler was able to study with Benjamin B. Warfield, one of Presbyterianism's intellectual giants and a leading apologist for Presbyterian Reformed theology. Ketler was graduated from Western in 1888 and subsequently ordained to the Christian ministry in the Butler Presbytery.

An evaluation of Ketler's education suggests that he aggressively sought ways to further his studies following his time in the London select school (grammar school), therein better equipping himself to teach. We may conclude that by the time he finished his theological studies in 1888, he had a solid education with both practical elements, normal school skills, and liberal arts components—Latin, Greek, theology, and philosophy. This served him well as he developed educational programs for Pine Grove's youth.

2. Educational Programs in Pine Grove: 1876-1910

If asked about the date of Grove City College's founding, most alumni and friends of the College would say it was in 1876. That, of course, is not accurate as recent books about the College clearly show. Grove City College was chartered by the Mercer County Court on November 21, 1884. Indeed, it was never referred to as a college before that date, not even by its visionary first leader Isaac Ketler. At that time a College seal was also created, a second version followed a few years later, printed on the back cover of this book. Some in the College family over the years have suggested that the College was an "idea" at least in 1876, but, that has no support in fact either, nor in the mind of Isaac Ketler.

David Dayton and Lee Edwards in his *Freedom's College* (2000) correctly note the founding date as 1884. Further, my examination of numerous publications by Isaac Ketler following his arrival in 1876 turned up no evidence of, nor claim by, Ketler that there was a college in Pine Grove in 1876. Indeed, he spoke of how well his academy/normal school was preparing students to attend "the nation's best colleges." If one thinks his school is a college, he does not say that he is preparing students to attend other colleges. Rather, he spoke and wrote about Pine Grove Normal Academy and published catalogues with that name on it until 1884. He expressed a desire to create a college in 1883. It's true that decades later some references to the College's origins do assume that it had roots in 1876. Such references do not, however, square with the facts that are rehearsed in this essay. On that point, consider the following.

We do have very good evidence, however, of what Ketler did once he arrived in Pine Grove until the College emerged in 1884. We can best understand what he did, it seems to me, by thinking of his programmatic efforts in education as a series of stages, as a kind of gestation before the College was conceived and then born in 1884. Since this development apparently has not been sketched out systematically, it will be helpful to do so here, especially since the process clearly displays the spiritual dimension of Isaac Ketler's educational efforts.

As noted in other accounts, Pine Grove had a "select school" for more than a decade before Isaac Ketler was hired in 1876. A "select school" was essentially a privately supported, grammar or neighborhood school, popular in the 19th century before universal education took hold. It was first operated at the request of a few Pine Grove parents by the Rev. W. T. Dixon and his wife. It met in their small home and later in the Presbyterian Church. The Dixons, however, decided to return to teaching at Sunbury Academy, nearer to Pittsburgh. Isaac Ketler emerged as the preferred candidate by the town fathers to replace the Dixons in 1875 or 1876.

By March of 1876 Ketler was hired and immediately circulated a flyer among communities in the area announcing the opening of a "Select School at Pine Grove." It would begin operating in April, the flyer noted. The flyer went on to say that the school's purpose was to "fit young men and women for college, and to prepare those who desired to teach to do good work in the school room." Like other select schools, probably like many earlier "one-room schools," it placed no emphasis on grade levels. Students from age six to twenty-one were accepted and at any time during the year, that is, not just on "the first day of school." Thirteen students enrolled the first day, some of these students apparently followed Ketler from the other schools in which he had briefly taught—New Hamburg and Scrubgrass Academy.

By the fall of 1876 the school opened with a new name, Pine Grove Normal Academy. That name tells us much about Ketler's plans, particularly the terms academy and "normal." The notion of "academy" at the time was that it offered a program meeting the practical needs students had for employment. Some of these academy courses were designed to support deficiencies in a student's select school experience, e.g., a course in decimals, grammar, elementary math, penmanship, and many more. It's important to recall here that levels in an academy tended to be ungraded. Ketler's academy soon offered "courses of study" and finishing the course of study was the goal. One of these courses of study in the academy curriculum had as its intention to prepare students to enter the "normal school" curriculum.

As for the meaning of "normal school" in the 1870s, it was viewed as a place with a curriculum that would show students how to teach, a two-year course of study as indicated above. One needed only an eighth grade level of study to be admitted. Obviously, when finished, a student would have a level of education equivalent, more or less, to the modern high school.

Ketler's school grew so rapidly—several hundred enrolled by 1879—that the trustees were moved to apply to the Mercer County Court for a charter. One was issued in April 1879 in the name that had been used for several years, "Pine Grove Normal Academy." The school continued to be operated as a private corporation whose stock was held by local citizens. In addition, several buildings were built to serve as classrooms.

The school was expanding at a dizzying pace because an ever-wider variety of programs and courses were offered. Hans Sennholz's study of the College's first 80 years provides us with a good way to understand the school's curricular structure by 1879. Expanding on what was said about academy and normal schools above, he says that Pine Grove Normal Academy was really three schools in one: an academy that offered courses for boys and girls not going to college nor into teaching; a high school that included college preparatory studies; and "a Normal School or School of Pedagogy" that provided training for elementary school teachers.

Evidence of Sennholz's characterization of the school's structure appears in its early catalogues. For example, a very wide range of courses were offered in the *Pine Grove Normal Academy Catalogue. . . For the Academic Year 1877-1878 and Calendar for 1878-1879* [included as Appendix B]. Latin, Greek, Practical Arithmetic (decimals and fractions), Spelling, Book-Keeping, Penmanship, and Ancient History are a few examples. Interesting, too, is the fact that the Academy had a very large music department. And, in a few years its Bible department boasted a strong summer program with several hundred students too. The school had a large "Primary" department which accepted students age 8-12, this being evidence of the size of the academy part of the school.

A striking feature of the curriculum of the school, on into its college years after 1884, is the continued proliferation of courses offered, courses of all kinds. One catalogue offered a course in telegraphy (telegraph key operation) with the advice that in difficult economic times (Depression of 1893) it would be a good trade to study because it had a future.

By the time the College emerged in 1884, the largest number of students, over 300, were enrolled in the normal school program. Interestingly, this teacher education program was referred to as a "scientific" program.

3. The Spiritual Dimensions of Ketler's Educational Efforts

Since our main interest here is in the development of the soul of Grove City College, we now focus on the spiritual life Isaac Ketler built into his educational program. The story is not surprising. From the first days of the select school in 1876, through the years of Pine Grove Normal Academy, on into the college years, Isaac Ketler assumed the basic tenets of Christianity to be the foundation of the school's curricular and devotional life. As we shall see, his own Christian faith matured during his years as head of the Academy and then the College.

A few quotations from catalogues will illustrate the point. The 1878 Pine Grove catalogue states the following on page 22 concerning "Religious Exercises":

> School is begun each day with devotional exercises. The chapel meetings are the most highly prized exercises of the school. Both teachers and students look forward to the morning meetings with pleasure. So strongly have the students become attached to these meetings that no effort is needed to secure prompt attendance. After the devotional exercises each morning, a half hour is spent in discussion of . . . the

biography of noted men and women, together with an analysis of their character and the elements which entered into the makeup of their success in life.

It continues with the following under the title "Prayer Meetings and Preaching":

Prayer meeting is held three times each week at the Presbyterian church and twice a week at the M. E. Church [Methodist], at which the students are always welcome. A number of churches of different denominations are within easy access of the school. Students are expected to attend preaching at least once on Sabbath. The influences with which students are surrounded are good. The morality of the town is proverbial. No licensed houses or saloons are in the vicinity. The location of the place is healthy and heartsome [*sic* wholesome].

The same message is re-stated in the first Grove City College catalogue of 1884, appearing in all subsequent catalogues including that of 1898.

As the century came to an end, the catalogues, since 1885 named *Grove City College Catalogue,* also discussed an ever-growing "Bible School." This was part of a huge summer school, *and* by the turn of the century it was the largest course in the summer program, drawing as many as 600 attendees, students as well as citizens from the community. Professors for the program included leading theologians, such as J. Gresham Machen from Princeton Seminary. Since typical attendees of the Bible School could ill afford the cost of travel, fees, and books, the session was always run at a loss. But, not ultimately. The record shows that Board Chairman Joseph Newton Pew paid all deficits for the Bible School session personally.

Catalogues also discussed "religious influences" in the school and town. Among them were the Presbyterian, Reformed, and Methodist churches. Special mention was also made of the Y.M.C.A. and Y.W.C.A. Catalogue discussions of "religious influences" summed up the topic by stating that "Christ is given a central place in all college enterprises." These provisions may be found in subsequent catalogues and are a testimony to the centrality of Christian thought, worship, and personal devotions in the life of Ketler-influenced institutions, from the select school on into the college years.

The same spirit is found in the 1927 document entitled, *The Charter and By-Laws and an Historical Sketch of Grove City College, Grove City, PA.*, Printed as *Grove City College Bulletin*, Vol. 19, January 1927, Number 1. For example, it cites with approval a September 1878 meeting of Pine Grove citizens, who were planning to erect a building for the school, in which presiding officer Robert Black said, "In view of the very great and vital interest which has brought us together, it is proper and wise that Divine guidance and blessing be sought." He prayed. The 1927 document also states that "the College shall be thoroughly Christian and Evangelical in character." It also provides for "DEVOTIONAL EXERCISES":

> Prayers shall be held in the chapel at the commencement of exercises each day in the week, except Monday; upon which

services, and also upon the public worship on Sabbath in the Chapel, all students are required to attend unless for some good reason excused.

Isaac Ketler's provision for worship, devotions, and prayer meetings during his tenure were enhanced by his own theological studies. Following his B.A., M.A., and Ph.D. studies, he embarked on a venture into theological studies in Western Seminary in Allegheny, a community situated to the north of Pittsburgh across the Allegheny River. Decades later it was merged with Pittsburgh Theological Seminary. During the years 1885-1888 Ketler was given time off each year by the Board to study in the Seminary. He was graduated in 1888 and soon was ordained as a Minister of the Gospel in the Butler Presbytery.

Ketler's studies at Western were significant for several reasons. First, it gave him an opportunity to enhance his own theological foundations as a Presbyterian. This included Luther, Calvin, William Perkins, John Knox, and the Divines of the Westminster Assembly. Second, while Ketler attended Western, leading contemporary Presbyterian theologians taught there. As noted earlier, the most well-known of these scholars was Benjamin B. Warfield, who subsequently moved to Princeton Seminary and is known in modern church history as a leader of the Princeton School of Theology. This time away from the rigors of running Grove City College to pursue his first love must have been a great delight for Isaac Ketler. In addition, these studies certainly improved his ability to run Grove City College's Ph.D. program in philosophy. On a more personal level, we can imagine that these studies helped him encourage the many other ordained ministers who taught on the College staff. And, there can be no doubt that Ketler's deep theological studies invigorated an already healthy campus spiritual life, that is, Ketler's theological studies further enlivened the soul of Grove City College.

4. The Spiritual Significance of *The Pilgrims* (1910)

The depth of Isaac Ketler's spiritual life, and by inference the spiritual life of the College, is clear from what has been said. But, there is another important chapter in Ketler's spiritual odyssey which may have grown out of his theological studies in Western Seminary. It is displayed in his 1910 publication entitled *The Pilgrims: An Epic Interpretation* (New York: Fleming H. Revell Company).

This book is both remarkable and unique. It's remarkable because it is a history lesson written in poetic form. It's unique because poetic history lessons are not found in Modern history, only as one might expect, in the age of Homer, that mysterious figure shrouded in Greek myths of the 8th century B.C.; or, in the writings of the 17th-century Puritan John Milton.

Isaac Ketler's "Introduction" to this book is appended to this essay so that interested readers can see for themselves his explanation for writing it (Appendix D). We can, however, summarize his argument here briefly. Indeed, such a summary is essential because his motivation is unquestionably deeply spiritual, therein contributing to our understanding of the soul of Grove City College.

As he says, the book covers 14 years of the Pilgrim movement, from the time of its founding in East England (1606), through its stay for a time in Holland under the leadership of John Robinson, amidst its perilous journey over the high seas in a small boat, to its settlement at Plymouth Rock in 1620. It was one of many "separatist" movements in England at that time, says Ketler, meaning that it desired to cut itself off from the Church of England because that church had not fully embraced the vision of the great Protestant Reformers of the 16th century, especially John Calvin.

Ketler's devotion to the Westminster theology was certainly evident in his up-bringing, in his structuring of his educational efforts in Pine Grove, and in his theological studies in Western Seminary. Yet, his book *The Pilgrims* is a capstone expression of his devotion to that faith. Consider his comments on the Pilgrims from his Introduction: "Calvin, and his doctrines, embodied their best thought and highest purposes. In sincere loyalty to God, and to the Reformed Faith, they renounced membership in the Church of England, and, acting on what they believed to be a divine prerogative, established an Independent Body, or 'Church Estate.'" Ketler then stated that what the Magna Carta had merely promised, Calvin and the Reformed Faith fulfilled, speaking, of course, of political freedom. J. Howard Pew had this in mind later when he said, "From Christian freedom come all of our other freedoms."

Very important to Ketler is the proposition that the political expression of Calvin's religious creed finds its best expression in "the general doctrine of the Sovereignty of God and the Equality of men." Ketler then continues a detailed discussion of how one should understand the teaching of Calvin, finding in it no real conflict with philosophical thought of his time; an understanding of Calvin's views, like Ketler had, are virtually unknown in our time. He also stated that "the story as here told, is, therefore, incidentally a defense of Calvin, and his creed."

Ketler defends his decision to write the book as poetry. The core of his view is that the essence of his faith, his spiritual life, indeed his soul, is a matter of the heart. That is to say, formal theology is important and useful, but the essence of faith ultimately flows from the heart. Such a view is not surprising for one in the Reformed tradition. Calvin's motto was not, after all, a logical proposition or syllogism. It was, rather, *Cor meum tibi, offero, Domine, prompte et sincere."* (My heart I offer to you, O Lord, promptly and sincerely.) Further evidence of Isaac Ketler's devotion to the Reformed Faith is the fact that he devotes Book III, "THE PILGRIM'S OLYMPUS," to an account of how Calvin influenced the Pilgrims.

He concludes his Introduction with a summary or re-statement of why he wrote in poetic form. That is to say, he could capture best the expression of his soul this way. In this, of course, we hear an echo of that tinge of pietism that was part of the Presbyterian tradition. And, he contrasts that with mere historical data that most accounts of the Pilgrims use, data that in the end is sterile and shallow when compared to the real meaning one can find in heartfelt poetic expressions.

D. An Era Ends: 1910-1915

Isaac Ketler and the Grove City College Board had reason to be optimistic about the future of the College as the school ended its first decade in the new century. The College was growing in all ways, literally. Others have chronicled that growth in detail. Here, however, we merely note that the student body grew, the curriculum expanded, many new buildings had been built, and that the school was financially sound—thanks to Joseph Newton Pew and his dedicated industrial friends. In addition, the spiritual life of the faculty and students was vigorous, thanks to the steady leadership of Board Chairman Pew and the indefatigable College President Isaac Ketler. But, as Ketler published *The Pilgrims* in 1910, the College's future was about to undergo several dramatic changes.

Board Chairman Joseph Newton Pew would succumb to a fatal heart attack in October 1912, while in his office in Philadelphia. The death of Chairman Pew was a great loss to the College. He had been a great benefactor of the College for years, enlisting his industrial friends in Pittsburgh to help too. Indeed without his beneficent efforts the College would likely have struggled for years in the backwaters of higher education, perhaps even failing in the end. As important was Pew's spiritual strength which greatly aided Isaac Ketler's work as President of the College. Eight months later, in June 1913, Isaac Ketler died of a ruptured appendix. Hours before he died he told his friends, "My philosophy and theology unite in teaching me the sovereign goodness of God, and I do not worry after I have done my best." In November 1913, Alexander T. Ormond was installed as the College's new President. Ormond was well-known to the Grove City community, having taught in its Bible summer school for many years. At the time of his appointment 65-year-old Ormond, tipping the scales at 300 pounds, was a Professor of Philosophy in Princeton University. Ormond was able to sketch out his plans for the College, but two years and a month after his appointment as College President, he, too, succumbed to a fatal heart attack while visiting his brother in Elderton, Pennsylvania.

What would happen to the College with such a dramatic loss of leadership in such a short time? Clearly, it was the end of one era and the beginning of another. Would the College survive? Who would be the new leaders?

Chapter 3
A Time of Challenges:
Weir Ketler's Presidency (1916-1956)

Friends and constituents of Grove City College all know that Weir Ketler came to the College's presidency at the tender age of 27 and served for 40 years. On reflection it is obvious that this era was consumed by major events in American history: World War I, the Great Depression, World War II, and the Korean Conflict. Each of these had a profound effect on the College and its soul. There were also numerous internal developments that challenged President Ketler's administrative skills, all of which affected the College's character and structure. How did all of these matters fare under President Weir Ketler's leadership? And, how was the soul of the College affected by the challenges of this era? That is the question explored in this chapter. Before turning to a discussion of these challenges, it will be helpful to characterize Weir Ketler.

A. Weir Ketler: Who was He?

Standard documentation of Weir Ketler's early life include the following facts. He was born in 1889, the second of Isaac and Matilda Ketler's four boys. He attended local public schools and was graduated from Grove City College in 1908. Apparently he was a good student because he was immediately hired by the College to teach math and history, probably in the grades that were part of the school's Academy division. Next, he spent one year at Yale University and obtained a second Bachelor's Degree. Upon returning to Grove City the next year, he again taught math and history.

Meanwhile his father died, and in 1914 the Board appointed him as an assistant to the newly installed President Ormond. As noted earlier, President Ormond died in 1915 and the Board immediately appointed Weir Acting President, and in June 1916 named him President.

Looking behind standard data about Weir Ketler's early years, it seems useful in assessing young Ketler's personality to ask what the effect of his father's prominence might have had on him. Several factors may help us understand this relationship. One of these is the "long shadow syndrome." It is a well-known psychological insight that parents with a powerful personality tend to shape, and more often than not, limit in some ways, the development of their children. There can be no doubt about the fact that Isaac Ketler was an exceedingly powerful, indeed over-powering, personality. Our characterization of him earlier suggests that. Moreover, as a hard-driving visionary Isaac Ketler also possessed remarkable physical energy—which he used to the limit. Most everyone knows a person like Isaac Ketler, a person who, without even realizing it dominates—not necessarily in a bad sense—whatever situation he is in.

Part of the "long shadow" would also include the obvious fact that young Weir's father was President of the College, and in that position was the leading citizen in the town as well. Add to that, the significant fact that father Isaac was also a preacher, a very powerful one. "Preacher's kids" often suffer from community behavioral expectations that are too high, indeed, unrealistic. This is certainly burdensome for the child; not living up to such expectations can re-enforce the effects of a father's "long shadow."

How does a boy grow up in these circumstances? Does he happily follow in his father's footsteps? Is it possible that if he did so, he did so reluctantly?

We know from many accounts that Weir Ketler was a shy man, that he preferred to be alone rather than in crowds of people. He also suffered for decades from severe migraine headaches. Anyone familiar with these knows how debilitating they can be. Further, he did not want to be the President of the College. Perhaps it was due to the migraines. He resisted the Board's first requests that he take that position, eventually acquiescing to their wishes. It's also interesting to observe that Weir did not follow his father into the Christian Ministry. His hope was to take a different path, one that would lead to the practice of law. But, that avenue was closed when his mother pleaded with him to return home from Yale after one year because, as she said, "Your father needs you."

In addition to being the son of the College's powerful, dynamic President, Weir by all accounts was a man of many gifts. His academic record indicates that he was a person with substantial scholarly talents. Moreover, he was versatile in the range of subjects he could teach—math and history at the same time, for example.

There appears to be no substantial biographical account of Weir Ketler. Thus, in addition to this brief sketch we will look for additional insights about him as we examine the challenges he faced during his 40 years as President.

B. Administrative Challenges: Times that Tried Men's Souls

Here we look at three areas that were especially significant challenges in the life of the College during Weir Ketler's administration. We take them up in succession as operational issues; as challenges to the College's spiritual life expressed in its traditional confessional theology; and as challenges to the College's long-standing student-behavior rules. The latter two focus especially on the health of the soul of the College.

As Weir Ketler took up his duties as President, he stated his vision for the College. At an annual alumni meeting in February of 1916 he said:

> The aim of our college should be to send out young men and women who not only have well-trained and efficient minds but who possess well-rounded personalities, who respond to high motives and who follow high ideals. Their lives should exemplify solid, vigorous, aggressive Christianity. We want no smug self-sufficiency, or critical hypocrisy. We believe in constructiveness, in men and women who have courage, who believe in right and who are not afraid to make a stand for the right in the moral and civic issues of life.

Translating these lofty goals into practical results would present Weir Ketler with very substantial challenges.

1. Operational Issues

Turning to operational topics, they were, indeed, substantial. First in importance were the two Wars and the Great Depression. Of course, all the historical details need not be rehearsed here, but each of these events had a causal effect on everything President Ketler faced during his 40-year tenure. In other words, they were the backdrop for Weir Ketler's entire administration. Their effect began immediately. As he took office in 1916, preparation for war was underway throughout the nation. At more than one point during the next three years, the survival of the College was at risk. For example, the Board discussed the possibility of shutting down the school for the duration of World War I. President Ketler questioned whether the College could be successfully re-opened if it were closed.

Meanwhile, the College asked the Government to establish a military unit [ROTC] on the campus, which it eventually did, but meanwhile the Trustees resolved to establish a military training program at its own expense. The Pew family bought the guns in August 1917, and then other supplies needed for the program. All male students were required to enlist in this program unless they were physically unable.

No doubt this development was a challenge for President Ketler, but not as demanding as the fact that the war soon depleted male enrollment. In 1915-1916 there were 217 full time male students. The next year there were 90. As noted, there was talk of closing the College down for the duration of the war because costs increased and income declined. Moreover, it was not practical to lower the number of faculty because some departments had only one instructor. And, without a doubt it would be difficult to find instructors once the

College was closed and re-opened. The College stayed open but borrowed money to meet expenses not covered by the tuition from students.

The practice of borrowing money ended up creating a debt of $150,000 by 1920. In today's dollars that would be some millions of dollars. President Ketler struggled to reduce that debt. Part of his effort included a drastic reduction in the number of courses offered. Faculty size was also reduced. Among the courses of study dropped was the Ph.D. program which had been offered for more than 20 years. Incidentally, this degree could be obtained without study on the Grove City campus. Eventually the music program, long a sort of crown jewel in the school's offerings, was reduced to a small department with only a few students.

An additional burdensome challenge for many years was the question of accreditation. Regional associations were established as the 20th century opened by state schools in an attempt to create uniform standards of quality among the great variety of institutions that had grown up since the Civil War. Moreover, states were establishing their own normal schools which, being tuition free, were a severe challenge to private schools like Grove City College. In 1920 President Ketler told the Board that the College needed to seek accreditation in order to be competitive with the state schools. By 1922 Grove City College received accreditation by the Middle States Association on Higher Education. Middle States did not review Grove City College's status for over 30 years, it occurring at the end of Weir Ketler's administration. As we shall see, the absence of this review had a deleterious effect on the College.

Remarkably, the College built a dozen buildings, during Ketler's administration, eight of them during the

1930s. Among them was the beautiful Harbison Chapel, a monument to the faith of its benefactors, discussed later.

Significantly, as Ketler moved into the 1930s, he was accompanied by a new Chairman of the Board of Trustees, J. Howard Pew. These two founders' sons joined hands and hearts to weather numerous operational challenges. By that time Pew had become enormously successful in leading Sun Oil. His attention to detail accompanied him to the Boardroom of the College. Ketler and Pew became good friends as well, often vacationing together with their wives.

Another operational challenge during the 1930s was the need to borrow money, just as they had in 1920, to finish building several of the eight buildings constructed during that decade. On the other hand, Sun Oil did not borrow money to continue its expansion during the 1930s. Students of the College's operational policies in recent decades know all too well that by that time, under J. Howard's leadership, the College did not borrow money. Indeed, "We are debt free" has been a mantra of the College ever since.

Another interesting fact, in light of the famous *Grove City v. Bell* case later, was the College taking government money to help pay student wages in the 1930s. The Federal Relief Administration funds helped pay students for work in the library, painting fences, and building roads on campus.

One more noteworthy event during these years deserves mention here, the building of Mary Anderson Pew dormitory, dedicated in 1937. It was named in honor of J. Howard's mother. This building not only provided an exquisite residence for more of the College's young women, but also was continuing evidence of J. Howard Pew's recognition of the value of women in society, business, and the life of the College. Earlier, he was the first Board member to insist on placing women on the College Board. Also, from day one to the present hour an unwritten rule has been that about half of the College's students were to be women. J. Howard's mother, Mary Anderson Pew, may be credited with this principle.

A curious and intermittently used practice during the Weir Ketler years was the creation of military units as part of the College's course of study. Even in the early days such units were created, used for a while and then decommissioned. As American involvement in WWI began, the request for the establishment of a military unit could not be honored immediately, though it eventually was.

The College also had contracts to train soldiers in its classrooms during WWII—hundreds of them. Very significantly, at the end of the war several hundred returning veterans also enrolled in the College. This was, of course, a boon to College finances. Moreover, many were married with children, and thus, did not fit into the traditional college scene, though they were usually very good students. These veterans embraced habits that tended to be an exception to the traditional rules of the College. They liked beer, and, generally they were excused from some College rules by default.

To sum up matters operationally, the College had numerous challenges during the Weir Ketler era, some of them severe enough to raise the question whether the school would survive. That was owed to Ketler's steady administrative skills and a competent and active Board of Trustees. By the mid-1950s the school was on a more prosperous path than it had ever enjoyed. Yet, when Stanley Harker's administration began, it was also clear that problems remained. Before turning to that topic, we look at the College's spiritual life during the Ketler years to examine the condition of its soul.

2. Challenges to the College's Soul, 1916-1956

When Weir Ketler became President in 1916, the College continued to embrace the sturdy traditional theological views preached by his father. The senior Ketler's views, stated forcefully in his book *The Pilgrims* (1910), were also supported by Joseph Newton Pew and the Board of Trustees. Isaac Ketler referred to these views as "Reformed theology" in the Introduction to that book. He could have, as noted in the Prologue, termed this view a Biblical worldview. We have also referred to them as Presbyterian Confessionalism. This perspective continued steadily well into the 1920s.

From the perspective of J. Howard Pew, however, appointing Charles MacKenzie as President in 1971 with a two-fold charge, it's clear that the spiritual vision of the founders had changed at some point. The conditions in which the soul of the College existed had been compromised. J. Howard referred to the founders' teaching as "evangelical" and challenged MacKenzie to restore it to the College's program.

This candid and profound evaluation of the College in 1971 raises several obvious questions. What theological/spiritual changes, if any, occurred during Weir Ketler's administration? Stated more specifically, we ask: How and when did the College slip away from Isaac Ketler's traditional Presbyterian Confessionalism?

The first thing to observe here is that a theological revolution was under way as the Weir Ketler administration began in 1916. Theological worldviews always change, but the Weir Ketler years coincided with a period of rapid change in the American Presbyterian theological world—Modernism was knocking at the door. This theological view was affected by the same factors that influenced other facets of America's intellectual climate. Principal among these was an embracing of the method of analysis popularly known as *scientific*, most obvious in American discussions of *evolution* and Darwinism. In theological circles, an equivalent was a kind of scientifically-based theology that sprouted in Germany early in the 19th century. American thinkers by the time of the Civil War believed the "new thinking" in Germany had to be studied. Thus, many curious American scholars either read German theologians trained this way or went to Germany to study with them. In due course, the results were attempts to modify traditional Presbyterian theology, hoping to make the new view compatible with traditional Confessionalism. The ideas which emanated from Germany resulted from the formation of Berlin University in 1810. Friedrich Schleiermacher—the "Father of Liberal Theology"—figured prominently in its origin. The founders established Berlin as the epitome of an Enlightenment university on the premise that no subject contained absolute truth—including theology. All subjects were to be taught utilizing the secular premises of the Enlightenment.

    Eventually, the contrast between traditional Reformed theology and the newer German-based thinking became obvious when they advanced from a simmering difference to a boiling one. Sweeping the smoke aside, the root of what was now a conflict between these views is captured in answers to the question of authority. From another angle, the question was: What is the foundation on which one builds his theology? For traditional confessional Presbyterians it continued to be the Bible. For the newer view, by 1900 called "Modernism," it was an extra-Biblical [beyond the Bible itself] scientific process. The technique of this attitude was often expressed in the term "higher criticism." In practice, this view meant that the Bible could be best understood when scholars used principles of the natural world, the world of reason and logic, and extra-Biblical history to interpret theological issues rather than the Bible itself. It was not uncommon for practitioners of this view to frankly state that the Bible is simply in error on dozens of facts, not to mention claimed theological errors found in the doctrines of particular Bible authors.

This theological revolution did not seem to disturb the traditional spiritual practices initiated by Isaac Ketler and his theological associates in the College for more than a decade. Evidence of this may be seen in the continuation of the same patterns of required chapel attendance each day, public worship on Sunday, and required courses in Bible. A sampling of College catalogues during the Weir Ketler years shows the same commitment to a Biblical basis for the College. Moreover, a sampling of the Bible Department faculty, usually only three persons at any one time, and courses they taught during these years, appear to be a continuation of the founders' Confessionalism.

Significantly, this view is evident in a 1927 document entitled *The Charter and By-Laws and an Historical Sketch of Grove City College, Grove City, PA.*, Printed as *Grove City College Bulletin*, Vol. 19, January 1927, Number 1, cited in the previous chapter. It endorses what had been said in a September 1878 meeting of Pine Grove citizens who were planning to erect a building for the school. Said President Black, "In view of the very great and vital interest which has brought us together, it is proper and wise that Divine guidance and blessing be sought." He prayed. The 1927 document also states that "the College shall be thoroughly Christian and Evangelical* in character." It continued with a listing of devotional exercises that were to be part of the College program, including morning prayers, Sabbath chapel worship, personal Bible study, and other spiritual exercises.

But, some cracks in the College's theological armor appeared by the late 1920s, a point evident by an examination of the seminaries the Bible faculty attended. In a few words, these seminaries were disposed to embrace Modernism and its extra-Biblical sources on the authority question.

For example, Princeton Seminary was split into factions on this issue, advocates of a traditional Reformed view leaving Princeton to form new Reformed seminaries that retained traditional Biblical authority. One illustration of this was the creation of Westminster Theological Seminary in Philadelphia in 1929. A leading Princeton professor, J. G. Machen, lead the way by resigning from Princeton and joining in the formation of Westminster. The name of the school reflects its commitment to traditional Presbyterian Confessionalism. Noteworthy is the fact that Machen had taught in Grove City College's summer Bible School for many years while a professor at Princeton.

During the late Weir Ketler years and also in the Harker years, many of the College's Bible Department professors were trained at Princeton and other seminaries that also sided with the Modernist view on the authority question. Among these were Pittsburgh Xena, Western,

---

* The term "evangelical" appears a number of times in this essay, sometimes seemingly in conflict with the Presbyterian Reformed tradition (Confessionalism). In the popular mind, as opposed to the sophisticated scholarly one, the basic principles of each are the same: authority of scripture, salvation by grace through faith in Christ's atonement, and more.

and McCormick seminaries. Some Grove City College professors also studied in Germany as well.

Such education probably anguished the soul of the College. Indeed, it may be argued that it fed one side of a latent spiritual warfare. It's worth noting here, as Lee Edwards points out, that the *Collegian* argued in a page-one essay that the churches should "get back to the Bible" instead of sponsoring dances in an attempt to gain new members. "Give us more of the Word," it said. As for piety, that other thread in the spiritual life of the College, the Bible Department's faculty seemed to be touched with a streak of it, piety also continuing as a prominent practice in the culture of the town for years, including upon our arrival in 1972. The overall conduct and manners of the faculty reflected a tinge of Victorian culture as well, evident in widespread support for the Temperance Movement.

Most theological training of the Bible Department faculty down to the MacKenzie era took place in schools in the Modernist mode. This changed when MacKenzie, following the J. Howard Pew mandate, replaced retiring Bible faculty from the previous decades with men trained in Westminster or one of its branches, or trained in other confessionally-oriented seminaries.

It's important to note here two additional points about the Modernist, seminary-trained faculty during the Ketler/Harker years. First, they were amiable Christian gentlemen, colored with a touch of pietism and Victorian morals—not bad qualities for a college professor. Second, apparently they had not been exposed to the newer Christian apologetics. This newer view was a kind of philosophical theology which taught a full-blown Christian worldview based on a recognition of Biblical presuppositions as its foundational principles, but more on this in the next chapter.

In the absence of vigorous theological reflection, the Bible Department curriculum devolved into a series of courses that were increasingly a matter of simple Bible study, useful for personal devotions but not much more. That is to say, students in such courses were not given intellectual tools to use in defending their faith in an increasingly scientifically-oriented society.

Though curricular practices in the department strayed from the founders' structured Confessional perspective, there was continuing evidence on the campus of the spirit of the founders. The outstanding example of this is the Samuel P. Harbison Memorial Chapel. Money for it was pledged by Harbison's two sons William and Ralph, both members of the College Board. Plans called for the location of the Chapel at the edge of the upper campus so that it was visible from all parts of the campus. After its construction and dedication in 1931, it was thought of as the center of the campus.

Only a visit to the Chapel itself can do justice to its beauty, but a few of its features can be mentioned here to whet the appetite for a visit to it. Its exterior is made of Briar Hill sandstone and Indiana limestone designed in the Gothic style. A striking feature is the French style spire or fleche. The interior is adorned with much carved oak, especially in the chancel.

From the point of view of the soul of the College, the most striking features of the Chapel are the imported stained glass windows. As David Dayton points out in his *'Mid the Pines*, "The chancel window is a Reformation window centered in the figures of John Wycliffe, John Knox, John Calvin, and Martin Luther." Under them is the inscription, "There is no Head of the Church but the Lord Jesus Christ." And breathtakingly, the nave window centers on a majestic figure of "Christ the Great Teacher." In addition, "the side aisle windows portray incidents in the history of the early Christian Church as well as incidents in the religious and educational development of the United States." J. Howard Pew, at the dedication of the Chapel in October of 1931, linked it to the school's early days. Observed Pew, "The dedication of this beautiful chapel emphasizes the ideals which have inspired the establishment and development of Grove City College." Any visit to the Chapel likely evokes a spiritual experience in the heart of the visitor.*

    Thinking about the soul of the College and the dedication of the Harbison Chapel, remarks by the then-Vice President of the Board, Rev. W. L. McEwan are instructive also. He observed that Samuel Harbison and Isaac Ketler were "kindred spirits" and worked together for the up-building of the school. As to the motives of the Harbison brothers who gave the money for the Chapel, McEwan stated, "The purpose of the givers was to enable the school to maintain its Christian standards." He continued, "Christian men and women are coming to regard the small, definitely Christian college as one of the best agencies for the extension of the Kingdom of God." As for the placement of the Chapel, he echoed what others noted: "This building is set in the most prominent place on the campus, and thus, witnesses to the fact that the Christian religion is at the heart of its life." Surely the spirit of those responsible for the planning and design of the Chapel reflect devotion to the principles of traditional Presbyterianism, like those embraced by Joseph Newton Pew and Isaac Ketler.

    It's clear that the motives of the financial donors of the Chapel, their resolve to go ahead with its construction in the face of a deepening economic

---

* Its beauty is captured in words and pictures in Dale Russell Bowne's *Harbison Heritage: The Harbison Chapel Story* (Grove City: Grove City College, 1989).

depression, and the striking Biblical themes in the windows, tell something of the strength of the soul of the College too. Dedicatory remarks only re-enforced this theme. Furthermore, those who have used the Chapel for the-more-than 75 years since its dedication as worshipers, and as that special class of people who chose the Chapel for their weddings, likely have a warm spot in their hearts from this experience. Indeed, for most, their souls are stirred when they recall their visits to the Chapel. Such is the effect of Grove City College's Harbison Memorial Chapel.

College rules and regulations, and an evolving tendency to not observe them, however, provide an understanding of the erosion of the College's traditional Christian perspective by the time President MacKenzie was hired in 1971. With this in mind, we turn now to a consideration of student life in the Weir Ketler years.

3. Manners, Morals, and Student Behavior in the Weir Ketler Era

Standards for student behavior changed rather dramatically during the Weir Ketler era. At first, student behavior continued to reflect the spirit practiced during the age of Isaac Ketler. We defined this as a spirit of piety. Piety assumes that "Christian faith is more an affair of the heart, a matter of morality and holiness in daily living" rather than "a matter exclusively of the intellect." Piety continued during the early Ketler years to be evident in the requirement of daily morning worship and devotions before class, in vespers immediately after dinner three nights a week, and Sunday worship in local churches. Personal Bible study and devotions were also encouraged. Moreover, College catalogues continued to note that these practices were an essential part of student life for years.

But piety cannot explain all College requirements for student behavior. By 1920 some College publications set forth rules for students, especially females that can only be understood as Victorian. Exploring this topic will shed light on what was expected of students for years until school requirements were relaxed or lightly enforced. Two practices will illustrate much of the mood of Victorian manners and morals.

Consider first the dress codes. Even before the Weir Ketler era, Grove City College women dressed rather formally. In public, females were expected to wear long dresses with a high collar, long sleeves, hats, and laced ankle boots. Carrying a sun umbrella would also be expected in warm weather. The strength of some of these practices can be seen decades later when I arrived on the campus to teach. I digress a moment to make that point.

Soon after our arrival in 1972, my wife received a phone call from the wife of the History department chairman inquiring about a time that would be convenient for them to come and "call" on us. Gathering her wits after being surprised by the request to "call" on us, she suggested a late afternoon hour a few days hence. At the appointed hour, the doorbell rang and she welcomed the couple. The wife's clothing was striking in my wife's view. It consisted of a rather formal dress, a hat, and white gloves. The Chairman was, of course, in a suit and tie. Having consulted with her socially-adept mother, she had prepared to serve them tea and cookies. "Calling on people and being served tea was an old Victorian custom," her mother noted. After an hour's visit, they left. In the ensuing days, we received several bouquets of flowers as welcoming gifts. Victorians, of course, also used flowers as a form of language or communication. Other faculty couples also asked to come and call. In Grove City, some Victorian social habits obviously died slowly.

In addition to female dress codes, Victorians attempted to place great restraint on all things related to matters sexual. A footnote here on the history of this attitude will be useful in understanding the College's rather severe behavior codes for its female students.

During the last part of the 19th century, there was an active campaign to define what produced good health. As it turned out, matters sexual were related to it. A principal figure in this movement was Sylvester Graham, a Presbyterian minister, and the inventor of the graham cracker. An enthusiastic follower of Graham was W. K. Kellogg, inventor of corn flakes. Eating their food was, of course, the foundation of good health. Surprising to the modern reader is their advertising. Their crackers and flakes, they said, were an excellent way to suppress "carnal desires"—a practice recommended by medical doctors, not to mention the traditional ethical teachings of pastors. Indeed, abstinence would be even better for one's health, they said. Presumably, one needed to eat even more crackers and flakes to achieve this goal.

And, how does one limit carnal desires among young people in college? If Graham and Kellogg were correct, students could be fed more of their crackers and flakes. In addition, dress codes resulted in the covering of female bodies from head to toe with frilly dresses, leaving to the male imagination what a female body actually might look like. While these practices might be helpful, there was another effective way to control an outbreak of carnal desire. Keep male and female students separated as much as possible outside the classroom; and, issue a book of rules that all female students were required to follow. Grove City College published such a book for years.

Lest there be any doubt about how these restrictions on behavior affected the soul of the College, consider the weighty matter of chastity. It was, indeed, one of the cardinal duties of Christian women—young and old. Adultery and fornication long ranked high on the list of evils among Christians.

Detailed rules regulating female clothing and behavior was viewed by College administrators as their Christian duty. Such rules were a way to aid young women in avoiding corrupting desires, and surrendering their chastity. Of course, the rules included much more than those that directly addressed meeting or consorting with male students.

An example of such College rules is Dean of Women Lory Cory-Thompson's *Customs, Rules and Regulations Governing Young Women Living in Dormitories* (1921). It is attached to this essay as an appendix (Appendix C). A few examples of its rules include the following:

> -It is not only requested but also expected that everyone have a dignified and quiet bearing both in and out of the Dormitories.
>
> -Walking with men on the Campus must occur only occasionally. . . .Walking with men off the Campus except on Broad Street in the center of town is strictly a Senior privilege.
>
> -When Sports are in progress, a reasonable amount of companionship is naturally allowed.

-Do not call from one floor to another nor talk out of the windows to anyone below.

-Permission for picnics and hiking must be obtained and chaperones arranged by the Dean.

-Ragtime and Jazz are not to be played on Sunday.

-Autoing is only by permission and chaperones must always be arranged for.

-Autoing in the evenings is not allowed.

It's obvious that these rules are very restrictive from a modern perspective. The College continued to issue such regulations for years.

Notice that there is no mention of the use of alcohol in the women's rules. And, what meaning do we attach to the fact that men did not have College-sponsored rule books?

Other factors colored student behavior during the Weir Ketler era. Consider the fact that the two wars dramatically lowered the number of men on campus. What would be the effect when this deficit was made up at the end of the wars with an avalanche of returning vets? Certainly the vets were older and probably more mature—at least more experienced in the "ways of the world," especially after WWII. These vets tended to ignore or circumvent "inconvenient" rules.

Probably nothing changed student behavior more than the initiation of fraternities. Some of that began at the end of WWI. Students then wanted national fraternities, but the Board was firmly opposed to that idea; however, they allowed local ones. While available records about their formation and purposes are not easy to uncover, it's clear in private records, as opposed to official College records, that at least some of them in the early 1920s purposely went out to form social groups that intentionally flaunted laws and good morals. Secrecy about these matters was a matter of honor and part of the beginning of fraternal relationships. As we shall see later, fraternities developed into the central social organizations on the campus with the return of veterans from WWII. Regulation of them by the Ketler administration seems to have been limited, probably due to a small and aging Student Affairs staff, coupled with the fact that many men either lived off campus or had access to local houses for social purposes.

Significantly, the College archivist confirms that records affecting student behavior all through the Weir Ketler era are thin. This includes comments in the *Collegian* and the content of reports to the Board by the College President.

Another factor in the first decades of the Weir Ketler era that certainly affected student social life was the spirit and mood of the "Roaring Twenties." It was a time of comprehensive change in American society probably unmatched until the 1960s. These changes included economic, technological, and psychological ones. Their arrival was evidence of a rapid growth in prosperity, the invention and sale of numerous home appliances—toasters, refrigerators, radios, and much more—and the grand-daddy of all technological changes, the mass production of automobiles. One writer noted the effect of the automobile by referring to it as "a couch on wheels that could be run off into the woods." Psychologically, the end of the Great War brought great relief as the boys were brought home and mass-marketing generated a sense of national community that had not existed before.

But, the Roaring Twenties had another, more personal side, too, especially when it came to young people, college-age young people. Consider for a moment the life of a Grove City College coed. Dean Thompson's book of rules for behavior attempted to fence off much of the outside world with its emphasis on piety and Victorian manners and morals. Indeed, the general rules and practices of the College did the same thing. Then, imagine our coed picking up one of the new Roaring Twenties magazines in a downtown drug store in, say, 1924.

What did she see? She saw young women with short hair, short skirts, and cigarettes in their mouths as they entered an "auto," on the way, a caption states, to a talking cinema. A handsome man is about to drive her away—with no chaperone. If a wave of excitement did not overwhelm her, it would be surprising.

She wondered as she closed the magazine whether she might be able to experience some of the things she saw in it. How much fun that might be! A moment's reflection, however, brings her back to reality, the reality that Dean Thompson and her rule book would not approve of any of it. Soon she discussed what she saw and how she felt with some of her female friends. Later, she talked about it with her brother who was a senior. In due course they plotted a way to go off autoing, as Dean Thompson called it, to see a talking cinema and try a cigarette and a glass of "bathtub gin." This they managed without being caught by Dean Thompson.

The point is that something like this happened at Grove City College as students tested the temptations of the Roaring Twenties' culture. Dean Thompson's Victorian rules eroded year by year, thanks to the growing impact of the Roaring Twenties.

Yet, piety seemed not to erode, at least officially during these years. The College *Catalogues,* Presidential Reports to the Board of Trustees, and other College publications displayed the same reverence for worship services, Vespers, personal devotions, and Bible study that had been present since the early days of the school.

What do we conclude about manners, morals, and student behavior during the Weir Ketler era? The College archives covering these years have limited evidence on student behavior. First, based on a lack of evidence, we can assume that the rambunctious parties associated with fraternities that continue to be part of College folklore even today, or imagination-based nostalgia, did not exist in fact in the early Weir Ketler era. They have their roots in the next generation. Second, the long-standing practice of piety, in moderation to be sure, continued in the Ketler era. Third, Victorian attitudes toward female behavior that were present before Weir Ketler took office, continued for some years. These continued in the face of a changing culture because Dean of Women Thompson, the quintessential Victorian, required it in her book of regulations. Fourth, Grove City College did not exist in a vacuum. Its life was touched by the rising cultural tide associated with the 1920s, that is, by the material advances available in mass culture (radios, autos, etc.) and styles in clothing, music, dances, entertainment (talking movies), and the kinds of novels available.

Part of the folklore of Grove City College among students is that there was a time of riotous living generated by fraternity life. Such a way of life would, of course, stir the soul of the College, perhaps even placing it at odds with the kind of ethical principles the College's Biblical Confessionalism required.

Was the Weir Ketler era the source of the legends and folklore about riotous fraternal life in the college? The evidence, direct and indirect, suggests that riotous social life did not begin during the early Ketler years. As indicated earlier, the large number of matriculating veterans following WWII brought their own social habits. They liked their beer. In addition, their social habits in general seemed "worldly" in the eyes of the protectors of Victorian cultural attitudes on the campus and in the town. These habits, as a practical matter, seem not to have been effectively throttled by the College in the post-war years. Not easily explained, however, is the fact that in the next decade before Dr. Harker arrived, fraternity social life had reached proportions that would certainly cause many a college-fraternity brother's mother to blush. But, more on that in a following chapter.

To sum up the Weir Ketler years, we note, first of all, that it spanned a significantly longer time when compared to other colleges' administrations. This can, of course, be viewed in a positive light by saying that four decades of uninterrupted leadership provides continuity and stability. It could also be said that excessive longevity inhibits change, innovation, and natural impulses of creativity. And, as noted, it was not just that Weir Ketler was in office for a long time. His administrative colleagues also held their posts for a long time as well.

We add, however, in summation that operationally the College faced many enormous challenges economically and in the end weathered them fairly well. The College ultimately remained solvent, built many beautiful buildings, and soon after the end of WWII rebuilt its student enrollment.

As for the soul of the College, confessionally it faced the threat of Modernism. How it fared in this matter would become clearer some years later. As for student manners and morals, a basic moderate piety continued until the end of WWII. The question of Victorian practices was in the end a matter of customs which means they had no serious moral import. That they slowly faded away left no scars on the souls of students.

We look ahead now to a changing of the guard, Presidentially speaking. And, that would constitute a challenge to the soul of the College.

Chapter 4
Stanley Harker Welcomes Modernity (1956-1971):
Spiritual and Otherwise

The life of the College, including its spiritual life, was far different at the end of Stanley Harker's administration than it was at the beginning. As in Chapter 3 we will measure these changes in terms of three categories; operational/structural developments, theological/confessional innovations, and the evolution of student manners and morals. Why the life of the College changed dramatically can be understood by focusing on factors such as the following: First, the College lost its academic accreditation by the Middles States Accreditation Association. This sad state of affairs was followed by the Harker administration working "overtime" to correct the reported deficiencies. Second, the radicalizing of youth culture on most campuses had a sort of echo effect among the College's students. Third, part of the dramatic series of changes in college life during the Harker years was due to the unique spirit, attitude, and vision he brought to the job. That he had a new vision for the College was evident in remarks he made when he accepted his nomination for the presidency, discussed below. His personal style also was evident in the personalities and ideas of some of the faculty he hired. There can be no doubt about the effect of Harker and his new staff's style. In a word it brought elements of Modernity to the College.

The word *modernity* used here is intended to distinguish the mood and assumptions about life in Harker's administration from those in the 40-year-long

Ketler era. We now answer the question: "Who was Stanley Harker?"

A. Meet Stanley J. Harker

Stanley Harker was born in Wrightstown, New Jersey in 1903 to Sara Ella and Stephen Douglas Harker. His father died eight months after he was born, immediately creating hardships for the family. His father had been a grain dealer and so his wife resolved to carry on that business even though she had no experience in it. Her daughter Mary, 8 years old when her father died, eventually married a physician/soldier who wished to return to his home near Sharon, Pennsylvania. They persuaded her mother Sara to join them along with son Stanley.

Stanley finished his last two years of high school in Sharon and matriculated in nearby Grove City College, graduating in 1925. While there, he met Dean Calderwood's daughter Helen, eventually marrying her. They had three daughters. The yearbook and College paper indicate that there seemed to be no event or cause that Stanley was not involved in. Following college, he went to McCormick Seminary in Chicago and graduated in 1928. Over the next years he pastored several churches in Ohio and Pennsylvania, earned a doctorate from the University of Pittsburgh in history, and wound up in 1951 as President of Alma College in Michigan. In less than five years, he helped grow Alma's student body by 40 percent, managed construction of several new buildings, improved faculty quality, and raised money to pay off the school's debt. 1956 found Stanley Harker being offered the presidency of his alma mater, Grove City College.

The circumstances of this offer are worth mentioning at this point because they offer a clue to Harker's relationship to the College's Chairman of the Board and to the character of his tenure as President. Stanley Harker, like Weir Ketler, wrote a brief piece that David Dayton includes in the Foreword to his book *'Mid the Pines*. Among other things, Dr. Harker noted:

> When I was invited to the presidency I accepted with great reticence. I knew that I could never agree with many of the views held by Mr. Pew. I told him very frankly how I saw the matter. He denied that he expected me to become his 'yes man.' He insisted that we could talk through and come to an agreement on every matter before taking it to the Board.

Harker made it clear that Pew assured him he could have whatever time it would take to discuss College matters with him.

As we turn to an examination of the College's development during the Harker years, we are left with the question: To what extent did President Harker ultimately agree with Chairman Pew and the Board? We begin by summing up operational/structural developments during Harker's administration.

B. Harker's Operational and Structural Challenges and Changes

As Harker took up his duties as President, he was met with a report from the Middle States Accreditation Association which denied re-accreditation. The College had been accredited in 1922 but had not been evaluated since. The list of weaknesses in the College's academics, staffing, and effective administration was long. They said, among other things, that classes were too large; that they lacked an intellectual challenge in many cases; too often they were taught by faculty that were too old and/or under-educated; that there were too few administrators, who were also old and overworked; and that the library was far too weak for college level classes. Interestingly, the chain of command in the administrative structure was "vague and inefficient," the Middle States Report concluded. Perhaps the most crucial criticism in the report was that the College had done a very superficial and uninspiring job of preparing for the Middle States visit. In the words of the evaluation team, the "grave inadequacy of the self-evaluation of the College … is shallow, evasive or non-responsive to many questions and inadequate or incomplete in response to other questions." David Dayton, President Harker's son-in-law, summed up this situation in these pithy words: "In other words, the buildings were beautiful, but the program to go with them was woefully lacking." Stanley Harker saw all of this as a challenge and set about to correct as many of these flaws as possible before the next Middle States visit, set for four years later. Harker initiated enough changes so that when the Middle States committee returned, they were much impressed by the number of innovations that had been made in such a short time. These included creating a department system, hiring more than a dozen additional faculty so as to reduce class size, making plans for a new library that could house up to 200,000 books—150,000 more than the College presently owned, and an increased library book budget that was to be used to buy up-to-date books for all departments. Equally important, Harker pushed for improvements in the curriculum of which he said "we can be proud." In addition, he called upon the Board to support higher pay because that is the only way "we can attract and keep a quality faculty." And, one more item here: Harker made plans to construct a new classroom building on the upper campus, subsequently named Calderwood Hall after the long-time Dean of the College and his father-in-law.

Additional changes by Harker included the construction of eight new buildings during his tenure, quite an accomplishment indeed. Several of these were in response to an increase in applications for admission. More student involvement in sports was encouraged as well as a program to improve varsity football and baseball. A college bookstore was opened on campus also.

As for the many other operational and structural changes under Present Harker, their details are found in other books about the College. It is important to emphasize here that Stanley Harker did many great things to improve academics, administrative structures, and the physical facilities of the College. What happened to the soul of the College while the plant and equipment were improved under Harker's administration? Since the early days of the College, its spiritual life has been expressed in a traditional theological/confessional dimension and in student behavior with a touch of pietism.

C. More Challenges to the College's Traditional Confessionalism

After examining the sketchy evidence of what happened to the College's traditional confessionalism during the early Weir Ketler years, we concluded that it essentially remained the same for several decades. It was, however, challenged by an alternative view of theology that crept into the College community through the type of seminary training the Bible department faculty had. That view we called Modernism. We noted, too, that the same kind of training befell the Bible faculty during the Harker years.

Harker's changes that affected confessional aspects of the College's life took several forms. Important to be sure was the immediate change of the name of the Bible Department to the Religion Department, the latter, of course, having a much broader meaning. The result seems to be that the number of Bible courses was reduced while the number in the broader category of "religion" was increased.

Other changes did not fit neatly into the confessional mode, they being more a matter of style. Early operational changes included ending Saturday morning chapel. After this change, chapel still met four days a week, plus Sunday night worship. Harker ended the Saturday session because he said that it interfered with social and athletic events in the afternoon and evening. Next, he ended the Victorian segregation of men from women in chapel sessions. The men had here-to-fore sat on one side and the women on the other. Now they could sit mixed with each other as, Harker said, they did in their home churches. These changes were dramatic, even revolutionary in the minds of the old guard faculty. What in the world, they wondered, would the students be doing in such a mixed seating arrangement? Harker made another dramatic chapel change. Attendance that had been taken by faculty in a notebook on an assigned seat basis would henceforth be taken by students turning in IBM computer cards at the end of the exercise.

Harker's changing style can also be seen in the first faculty dinner at the beginning of the fall of the 1956 school year. In the minds of the old guard there were theological overtones to some of the President's actions and comments. Upon finishing dinner, some new faculty lit up cigarettes to the shock of spouses of older faculty. One such dowager vigorously scolded a smoker, stating, "No one smokes in here except Mr. Pew." Pew smoked hefty Cuban cigars. No doubt it was an absolute shock to that faculty wife when President Harker soon stood to address the faculty, puffing on a large black cigar. Tinged with a streak of piety that yet lingered on the campus, she wondered out loud how an ordained minister could do that. She probably wondered to herself whether this cigar-smoking President went so far as to drink beer, or heaven forbid, liquor. Chances were, too, that she was, like many faculty wives, an active member in the local chapter of the Women's Christian Temperance Union.

At the same faculty dinner-meeting, President Harker spoke about the nature of a Christian college. As was becoming evident, he spoke rather bluntly: "A Christian college is not characterized by piety," he said, "but rather by demonstrated excellence in its academic programs." Diminishing the place of piety in College life surely made old-guard faculty uneasy. Indeed, that comment likely was even more unsettling when President Harker stated that "terminal degrees" (a Ph.D. degree or its equivalent) were a mark of a high quality faculty. There were few terminal degrees, nor had there ever been, among the faculty.

An additional observation by President Harker was at least an oblique comment on a theological confessional perspective. Harker insisted that "in our search for truth, we must objectively pursue all viewpoints on our campus, living within our heritage under a Christian umbrella." This stance was a far cry from what Harker must have heard in his Grove City College classes during the early 1920s, the word *objectively* being the key. The principle of "Biblical authority," so pervasive in earlier days, seems absent from Harker's observation. Further, this seems like evidence of what Harker meant when he said at the time of his hiring: "I knew that I could never agree with many of the views held by Mr. Pew." Pew was, of course, an outspoken defender of the proposition that "the Bible is the infallible and authoritative Word of God." Pew started with the Bible as the source of truth, while Harker implied that truth might be found in searching "all points of view." In Harker's mind this included Modernism, the view that sources above and beyond the Biblical one were to be honored as well. What Harker's "Christian umbrella" was, is not clear.

An item or two here will conclude these observations about "additional challenges" to confessionalism during Stanley Harker's administration. One involved a changing of the content of chapel exercises. During the first 70 years of the College, chapel was marked by 45 minutes of singing, Bible reading, meditative reflections on great Christians, and prayers—all marks of traditional piety. By the end of the Harker years it was reduced in time to 10-15 minutes. This would include a song or two and then a reading of a Bible passage. Very significantly, the Bible reading was done without comment. The exercise concluded with a prayer and the singing of the Alma Mater.

The College Catalogue stated that the Chairman of the Religion Department was the "College Pastor," which did not appear to have any particular significance. An interesting incident concerning this position took place at the end of Harker's Presidency neared. As we shall see in detail later, J. Howard Pew realized that much about the College's spiritual life had changed by the late 1960s. He resolved to return it to its traditional theological stance. One measure he took was to hire a full-time chaplain for the College. In discussing this plan with Allen Bell, one of his close Sun Company advisors, Bell made a suggestion. His church had a wonderful pastor who would be just right for the College's students.

This Pastor had been a circus performer for some years before becoming a Christian and going on to seminary training. He served as a pastor in the Associate Reformed Presbyterian Church in the South, which is known for its deep commitment to the Westminster Assembly tradition. Its foundational idea was exactly that held by J. Howard Pew—the infallible authority of the Bible. After an interview, J. Howard hired him to be the College chaplain in 1969, only announcing this to President Harker after the fact. The new chaplain's name was Jack Heinsholm. Since this appointment was an unplanned addition to the College staff, Pew paid his salary.

This was apparently another one of those times that Harker, as he said, "Absolutely could not agree with Mr. Pew." Heinsholm was not warmly received by President Harker upon his arrival in Grove City.

Pastor Heinsholm arrived as school opened, prepared to run chapel services based on meditations flavored with his experiences in the circus—an approach he thought would go over well with the students. When President Harker got word of Pastor Heinsholm's intentions, he said, "That is not the way we do it here," reciting the fact that they just read a passage from the Bible without comment, made a few announcements, sang the Alma Matter, prayed and went to class. In due course, Heinsholm had his way, especially in the Sunday evening services. He packed the students in! They loved his style and performance!

When it came time for contracts to be renewed, one of Heinsholm's fellow Religion Department professors asked him if he got a contract. It was now two weeks after all the other faculty had received theirs. "No," was his reply. When word was out that Pastor Heinsholm would not be back the next year, students signed a petition asking that he be returned. About 1,400 of 1,900 students favored it. When the President was asked by Mr. Pew about why Pastor Heinsholm was not returning, the record shows that President Harker told Mr. Pew that 1,400 students in a petition <u>opposed</u> his return. It was the summer of 1970. In a year, Harker was retired and Charles Mackenzie became the next President of Grove City College.

D. Changing Student Manners and Morals in the Harker Years (1956-1971)

1. In General

There can be no doubt about the fact that President Harker greatly improved the academic side of life in the College, beginning these improvements soon after he arrived. His retrieval of accreditation from Middle States speaks to this achievement. In addition, Harker initiated certain changes in customs and style in faculty practices that pulled the College further away from quaint Victorian-like, 19th-century practices that had continued well into the late Weir Ketler years. When it comes to the question of student manners and morals under President Harker, a different story emerges. It must be viewed in a larger context, one that takes into account evidence of student behavior in the previous administration and in the one that followed.

Our earlier account of student behavior during the Weir Ketler years mentioned a continuing echo of traditional piety, a flourishing Victorian sub-culture for some years, and then the impact of the Roaring Twenties on the spiritual and social life of students. An important qualifying observation in that discussion was the fact that evidence to support any evaluation of student life during those years was modest.

There is much evidence of a well-developed, expanding, even strenuous, party life at Grove City College as MacKenzie assumed his Presidential duties, including records of the Student Affairs Office, Presidential reports to the Board, articles in the *Collegian*, yearbook presentations, and numerous students' testimonials about the nature of party life. Perhaps the most important key, however, to understanding change in social philosophy and student behavior during the Harker years is to be found in the work and writing of the last person Weir Ketler hired in 1956, Dr. Fred Kring.

2. Dean Fred Kring's New Style

Before outlining Kring's policies and practices, it will be useful to sum up his background. This data, and most of what can be known about his views, may be found in his 1988 book entitled, *One Day in the Life of Dean Fred: Autobiography or Legend*.

Fred Kring was born in Somerset County, Pennsylvania, in 1919. He tells us that his family may be traced back four or five generations into Swiss and German communities, which consisted of the practicing

Amish—at least until his generation. His family was basically small-town and back-country in location and culture, residing in Davidstown. He was near enough to Johnstown to attend high school there. As he finished secondary schooling in 1937, he was not certain what he wanted to do, though he notes in his book that he was disposed to become a teacher. With the help of a local teacher he applied to Millersville Normal School and was accepted. There he did well as a student and met Hilda Adam, whom he later married. After college he taught for a few months and was soon drafted to serve in the Army, just days before Pearl Harbor. After much schooling in the Army, he wound up in the Pacific Theater, his service ending in October 1945. During the next few years he taught in several high schools and finished work on a master's degree; finally he finished a Ph.D. in Educational Psychology at the University of Pittsburgh. During the spring of 1956, Kring was interviewed by President Weir Ketler for a teaching position at Grove City College. A job was offered and Kring accepted.

     A year later, President Harker offered Kring an additional half-time appointment as Dean of Men. Women had their own Dean. Thus began his long stint—including several as Dean of Students—in college administration. Kring tells us that he had no job description, but that President Harker wanted a dramatic improvement in student **morale**. "From where we are, Fred, the only direction we can go is up." Harker also suggested to Kring that they be restrained in disciplinary actions—this in light of the fact that under the previous regimes, strict discipline was the order of the day. As we shall see, a new order was about to begin in student life, and thus, in the nurture of the soul of the College.

Ask yourself while reading the following pages: What would J. Howard Pew and the Board of Trustees think of student behavioral practices that developed during this period? And, did these practices improve the quality of the soul of Grove City College, or not?

A careful study of Kring's book shows no evidence of elements associated with the College's traditional confessional theological stance. Further, there is no evidence of Christian, that is, Biblical ethics, and no mention of Christ, not as the Redeemer/Savior of believers, nor even mention of Christ as a "good man." In fact, there is no mention of an appreciation of Christianity in even its broadest cultural form either.

Instead, Kring's book displays a steady drum-beat of criticism of the College and its traditions, including those touching student behavioral requirements. Kring had never set foot on a Christian college campus, attending only public colleges and the University of Pittsburgh, a quasi-public institution at the time he matriculated there.

Significantly, Kring's own family background was Amish, but by the time he was a small boy, all that was left was a small jot of it. His theology, he says in his book, was a "peasant theology" that he learned in a Sunday school to which his mother took him early in his life. Like much in his book the "peasant theology" statement has several levels of meaning. For example, he wants the reader to know that his theology was simple and personal, and therefore, in contrast to the sophisticated and complex theology of the College's Presbyterians. Kring does state that his wife was Lutheran in background. Grove City townspeople knew that Hilda Kring was active in the local Lutheran church. There does not appear to be evidence, however, that Fred was active in this church.

In place of any reference to the College's traditional theological views—views that Isaac Ketler called "Reformed"—Kring espoused a worldview that can only be called "humanistic." This is evident in a persistent theme that runs through Kring's book and lifestyle, that is, that man (read students) is essentially good. His humanistic worldview can be inferred from his graduate studies in psychology. He readily quotes from leaders in this field, such as Carl Rodgers. Thus, his standard for ethical behavior for right and wrong for students was not Biblical ethics. Right and wrong were, rather, based on each particular situation. This view is, of course, called "situational ethics." Kring's application of this view is evident in dozens of events recorded in his book.

Some examples of how Kring handled student issues will show how his humanistic, situational-ethics philosophy worked out in action. It's noteworthy that once Harker had appointed Kring as the Dean of Men, Harker left most disciplinary matters up to Kring. And, when student behavioral issues came to Harker, he almost always supported Kring's decisions.

There is no doubt about the fact that serious beer drinking parties began by the end of WWII at Grove City College. As stated earlier, returning vets certainly contributed to this practice. They were, after all, older and much more experienced with the broader American culture. It's noteworthy, too, that the student population was increasingly less Christian in outlook. Some of this may have been the result of the need for students by 1945 because half of the male students in 1941 went off to war. In other words, an easy admissions policy may well have been in place as the war ended.

When Kring became Dean of Men, students soon learned that Kring was not only very tolerant of their beer parties but actually encouraged them. Kring tells us in his book that he frequently rushed to the police station, or to the State Police barracks, to head off the arrests of students for underage drinking. Beer drinking seemed to be of three types. Casual drinking in the dorms, more serious regular drinking in off-campus, frat-run houses, and also planned mass (hundreds of students at a time) drinking parties at remote farms, state parks, and also at the Kring "farm" just east of town. Women were frequently present at these parties as well. And, when College coeds had to return to their dorms by curfew time, it was common for town girls to join the men at parties.

Eventually, serious liquor use and drugs became part of student party habits. Some of it occurred in the frat houses. Kring tells us, however, that his wife at holiday time served two kinds of tea to students—one was mixed with whiskey and a second with gin. It was also common in warmer weather for coeds to sit out on their own smaller, secluded quad lawn in their swim suits and sip rum and coke. At other times, when they were fully dressed, they would sit out on the large quad and sip the same drink or some variations of it. Men often joined them on these occasions.

Kring's book shows that he thought sexual encounters without benefit of marriage between young males and females was a normal and healthy practice. There were, of course, school rules against this. In time, the frat houses served as the sites for many such encounters. Moreover, it was expected that at Spring Parties students would often plan on private encounters at motels and homes far from campus. Not all students took part in these outings, but it was a common occurrence in some fraternities and sororities. This practice continued well into the 1980s.*

Kring also prided himself on the practice of several psychological techniques. It appears, however, that he was not "Board Certified" to practice them for profit. Nevertheless he tells us that he regularly practiced hypnosis and therein, he says, cured numerous students of various phobias. Once he returned to the faculty full-time in 1973, he joined other faculty in advancing various forms of group therapy. One of these involved a student telling the rest of the group any and everything that troubled him. Another involved the group all lying on the floor and touching each other's feet in a séance fashion.

Kring also writes that he spent much of his time sitting in the GeDunk dispensing advice to students, often late into the evening.

A final example of Fred Kring's attitude towards student behavior should focus on what he says he learned about student behavior when he was asked to be an advisor for a popular fraternity, a year after he became Dean of Men. The brothers explained to him, he says, how they collected hundreds—if not thousands—of course papers from virtually every department. If a brother did not want to write a certain course paper, he could look in these files and likely find one he could turn in "as is" or modify it a bit before turning it in as his own.

This practice is commonly known as cheating through plagiarism. Kring referred to this as part of the "underground curriculum." It appears that the practice went on for years, on into the MacKenzie years. Failure

---

* My wife was a sorority mother at that time and was strongly urged to discourage the women from making reservations after Spring Parties.

to report this practice by an administration official would strike most people as ill-advised.

Looking back at a question posed at the beginning of this discussion, we ask again: From a Christian perspective, was the soul of Grove City College improved during the years Fred Kring was Dean of Men/Students, or not?

E. Harker's New Faculty

We noted earlier that one severe criticism of Grove City College by the Middle States Accreditation Association was the small size of the faculty in proportion to the size of the student body. We noted, too, that President Harker moved quickly to hire more faculty, a dozen or more in a hurry. Yet, the hiring process was constrained when it came to hiring faculty who had substantial graduate work. Thus, most of the new faculty held master's degrees only and many of these were hired away from local high schools.

Significantly, from the point of view of the spiritual life of the College, most of the new faculty were in the mold of Fred Kring. A few had graduated from Grove City College, but that would mean that they had matriculated at a time when the soul of the College, either in its theological dimension or its student behavior aspects, was weak. Other new faculty had been trained in public institutions or a few in other private colleges. It appears that a few of Harker's new hires were actively in the Christian tradition of the founders. Others gave no evidence of holding a Christian worldview at all. Many were, of course, good teachers of the data content of their field of study and teaching.

Most of the new faculty, naturally, were much younger than the existing faculty. That fact alone would suggest that they would have fewer attitudes and traits—like elements of piety and Victorian habits—of the older faculty. Evidently, this created some tension between the older and newer faculty. This implies that many newer faculty, certainly not all, were disposed to hold some of the same attitudes towards student behavior as those espoused by Dean Kring. Kring tells us that he readily made friends among Harker's new faculty; many of them were frequent guests at Kring's house.

As the MacKenzie era began, Kring was re-assigned to full-time faculty status. Kring and some of his friends hired by Harker 15 years earlier coalesced into a group that single-mindedly opposed MacKenzie's reforms and the new faculty he hired. This opposition rose to the level of being spiritual warfare, that is, a battle between worldviews, a battle between rank humanism and a Biblical perspective. Such was the relationship between Kring and his allies and most of the faculty MacKenzie hired.

We turn now to the MacKenzie era. It began in 1971 and some thought the changes he was asked to make by J. Howard Pew would take 5 to 10 years. In fact, it took most of 25 years—until about 1995. The changes fundamentally altered the school. It became again what it once was, a Christian College. Significantly it also achieved a much higher level of academic quality with a unique Christian perspective on faith and learning.

Chapter 5
"Gentlemen, We are Going to Recapture our Christian Principles."

Introduction

We have mentioned the MacKenzie Era several times already in this essay, the point being—stated or implied—that it ushered in a new age for Grove City College. The key event that began this new era, also noted several times, was the challenge that J. Howard Pew presented to Charles S. MacKenzie as he offered him the College's Presidency in 1971. To emphasize, Pew said: "Return the school to its Evangelical (read theological/Biblical) principles in the classroom and clean up student social life." Stated another way, this meant re-establishing a Biblical perspective in the intellectual life of the College and re-establishing Christian ethical principles in student life.

From the point of view of this essay, President MacKenzie was to revitalize the soul of the College—to revive the College's spiritual life, in both the classroom and in student life in general. This is a factor we shall keep in mind as we trace development in this era.

MacKenzie and the Board of Trustees took up Pew's challenge. Lee Edwards sums up their view of the matter in his *Freedom's College*. Nothing less than the soul of the College was at stake. States Edwards, "The overriding issue for the MacKenzie administration was the spiritual environment of Grove City College," based on MacKenzie's first report to the Board in 1971 in which MacKenzie said that the College "stood at a crossroads." Edwards then observed that "humanistic and Christian forces were contending with each other for control of the school" and that "secular humanism had made deep inroads into the College's life." Reflecting MacKenzie's report to the Board, Edwards notes that if allowed to continue, it could soon alter "the philosophy and historic position of the College." Referring, no doubt, to immediate faculty changes MacKenzie made, Edwards quoted MacKenzie's observation that "strong Christian forces were struggling to hold the College on course."

Another way to appreciate President MacKenzie's observation that the College "stood at a crossroad" is to look at the issue from the point of view of spiritual warfare. St. Paul talks about it often in his writings. Consider what he says in II Cor. 10. We are not involved primarily in physical warfare, he says, rather Christians are involved in spiritual warfare. Our weapons are spiritual and intellectual. The battle is between the forces of good and the forces of evil, between light and darkness. In this passage, St. Paul specifically calls upon believers to "cast down vain imaginations and everything that exalts itself against the knowledge of God ...," and he goes on to command us to "bring all of our thoughts captive and obedient to the will of Christ." Here he clearly points out that some knowledge is opposed to what God requires, while some is consistent with His will and plan. Practically, this means that some ideas taught are not consistent with the will of Christ while others are or can be. Knowledge is not neutral. Its truth or falsity is ultimately measured against the mind of Christ, which is reflected in the Scriptures.

Christians are always involved in this struggle. And, we say with emphasis here, that Christian institutions are also involved in this struggle. In my view, this essay is a chapter in the history of spiritual warfare. No Christian institution develops in a straight line from its roots through the decades and longer without spiritual struggles, yes, spiritual warfare. Indeed, if a Christian institution gains some high ground in this struggle, it likely will be tested by the forces of evil. There will be a struggle for the soul of the institution.

Significantly, Edwards quotes MacKenzie's statement to the Board that "a committed and determined Board of Trustees would be the deciding factor in this struggle." The Board responded with a Statement of Identity, which restated the College's calling as a college "thoroughly Christian and evangelical in character." Importantly, the Board also approved a program of faculty development that focused on hiring new faculty with "deep Christian convictions." Here we see the intention of the Board, under the leadership of Albert Hopeman, to improve the spiritual life of the school. MacKenzie also added at the time that he thought the struggle in the College reflected one "for the soul and identity of the nation."

Edwards next pointed out, with some understatement, that "the administration's emphasis on evangelical Christianity and the need for moral conduct on and off the campus triggered a strong reaction among some students, faculty, and staff." MacKenzie, shaken by the strength of opposition to his new programs, sought advice from retired President Weir Ketler. Ketler recounted how early in his administration students had threatened to go on strike. Ketler assembled the students in the Chapel and said to them in a calm voice, "My father started this school with 13 students. If necessary, I will start over again with 13 students." There was no student strike. MacKenzie was heartened by Ketler's courage and principled stand, he said.

It's worth observing in passing that in 1970 as MacKenzie was hired, J. Howard Pew likewise gave serious consideration to urging the Board of Trustees to shut the school down and begin again. Such was his shock at what he had seen and heard about the school's intellectual and moral climate. He was dissuaded from taking this action by certain long-time Board members.

In earlier sections of this essay, we looked at intellectual/curricular and student/behavioral dimensions of college life as we evaluated the spiritual life of the College. Revisiting these topics here will give us insight into the gravity of the challenges MacKenzie faced. But, here we also add a new element for consideration—the nature, scope, and extent of faculty and student opposition to MacKenzie's reform agenda. We examine curricular changes first because they began soon and had far-reaching results.

Curricular Reforms

For decades Grove City College, like dozens of other institutions, had a curriculum that required students to take a wide range of courses along with a concentration in a major field of study. This range, of course, was a sort of sampling of fields—a course in each of various departments. Beginning in 1973, this system was replaced with an 18-hour core program, called the Keystone Curriculum; six hours in religion/philosophy, six hours in humanities, three hours in social science, and three hours in the physical sciences. In addition, 30-38 hours were taken in a major field of study. This left time for students—in most majors—to also take cognate and elective courses. A decade and a half later the core concept was expanded to 32 hours at President Jerry Combee's suggestion.

Though planning for the Keystone Curriculum began soon after MacKenzie called for curricular changes, it took some years before all phases of it were implemented. Moreover, the results were uneven as far as Christian perspectives on learning were concerned. A central difficulty was finding and/or selecting faculty who were equipped by training, temperament, and commitment to teach from a Christian perspective. MacKenzie viewed the religion/philosophy course as the cornerstone of the whole core program. As for staffing it, faculty slots opened up as several senior faculty in the old Bible/Religion Department announced their retirement. Two additional faculty were also immediately hired to help design the religion/philosophy course.

Since the religion/philosophy course was intended to be the foundation conceptually for other courses in the core program and in the College at large, we will look at it in detail first. It's evident in looking through recent College *Bulletins* that the religion/philosophy course has deeply influenced the College's curriculum for decades. Next, we examine the Creative Keystone course in some depth because it was also a year-long course and because of its effect on the soul of the College.

The Social Science and Natural Science Keystone courses will be briefly considered following our evaluation of the Creative Keystone course. Why? These courses had difficulty because few faculty were available who understood and embraced a Christian perspective on learning in these fields. In other words, it took years to find faculty who could help move them into a position where a Christian perspective was possible.

A. The Religion/Philosophy Keystone Curriculum

It's important to observe here that J. Howard Pew's desire that orthodox Christian principles be reestablished in the College was not a reactionary request for a knee-jerk return to the views of the College's founders; nor was it a desire for the creation of a simple, plain-spoken, "no-creed-but-the-Bible" view of life, nor was it a matter of establishing a Fundamentalist Bible college. Such disparaging anti-intellectual remarks were made at that time by faculty devoted to the "man is the measure of all things" philosophy of humanism. And, the remarks were intended as a "put down," inferring that the Christian emphasis in the course was nothing more than a warmed over Bible college curriculum. Proponents of these remarks were obviously faculty who opposed a Christ-centered worldview. If they had read the course outline or heard some of its lectures, they would have realized that the course's content was a sophisticated philosophical defense of the Christian faith, of the Reformed/Presbyterian confessionalism of Isaac Ketler. Significantly, during the early years of the rel/phil course, some faculty assigned to it stated that studying to teach it stretched them more than most of their Ph.D. work had. Critics would have realized, further, that it was taught with a practical application, teaching students (like the new President Paul McNulty '80) how they ought to live and think.

    J. Howard Pew knew exactly what kind of change he wanted in the intellectual life of the College. He was an accomplished student of the Westminster Assembly's work, a point noted in Chapter One of this essay. Like the founding President of Grove City College, Isaac Ketler, who also was J. Howard's college professor, he saw himself as a devoted supporter of the theology of the Westminster Assembly. It was this perspective that was naturally in his mind, and he understood that its basic doctrines were the same as those embraced by his friend Billy Graham.

The Graham movement was, of course, usually characterized as Evangelical in the public arena. "Reformed" and "Evangelical" have been used to describe the perspective of Grove City College throughout its history. For many people, the terms are roughly synonymous and characterize American denominations that were orthodox in their Biblical theology and practice in the 18th and 19th centuries. Another term used in the 20th century to describe conservative views is "Fundamentalist." The College from its inception has never described itself as fundamentalist, never using the term in its literature nor in its public statements.

As noted above, success in the new religion/philosophy course depended on assembling a faculty capable of designing and teaching it. Various members of the old religion faculty suggested that a series of topics in religion would be a good idea. Meanwhile, President MacKenzie interviewed candidates outside the College faculty who could help design the course. During his first year on the job, MacKenzie hired new faculty members and the first two were hired to help with the development of the religion/philosophy course. In this, President MacKenzie was an outstanding facilitator. He made it possible for its creators and those faculty who followed them to embrace a new Bible-based, Christian perspective on learning—that is a worldview.

We turn now to a consideration of the religion/philosophy course itself. This account will first describe how the course was created, then it will examine basic concepts that gave the course its structure—many found in the Bible itself, thereafter outlining some methodological factors, and sum up the cultural eras the course covered. From these observations a good, though brief, summary of the course's Christian perspective, Christian worldview, will emerge. Readers should be alert for discussions of some new or unfamiliar terminology—such as, "worldview," "presuppositions," "cosmogony," "cosmology," "epistemology," "pre-theoretical," and more.

How was this course on Christian perspective on learning created?

The initial design of the course was the result of efforts by Ross Foster, Andrew Hoffecker, and John Van Til. Foster was already on the Grove City faculty for two years and had been trained in the Reformed Episcopal Seminary and Temple University Graduate School, both in Philadelphia. His special fields were ancient philosophy and logic—the latter with emphasis on epistemology (the problem of knowledge: How do you know you know?). Hoffecker was the second of the two new faculty members hired by MacKenzie to help with this. His studies following Dickinson College included Gordon Conwell Seminary and Brown University Graduate School. His fields were history of philosophy and theology and American Presbyterianism with a focus on the "Old Princeton" theology. Van Til, the other of the two new faculty MacKenzie hired for the religion/philosophy course, grew up in the Dutch Reformed tradition and studied Dutch Reformed philosophy at Calvin College. His additional graduate studies included law, ancient and medieval history, and European and American intellectual history with a focus on Puritan studies.

After many discussions among faculty assigned to the religion/philosophy course, Foster, Hoffecker, and Van Til met numerous times at Van Til's home to sketch out an outline for the course, based on their common experience as scholars in the Reformed tradition and their desire to cobble together material for a Christian "worldview." Since "worldview" became a central concept in this course, it will be helpful to pause here and explain it.

Philologically (a word's history), it's clear that the term is a derivative of the German word *weltanschauung* (literally, "world perspective"), first used by Immanuel Kant in his *Critique of Judgment* in 1790. Other German writers used it and Americans, like William James, were using "worldview" by the end of the 19th century. The term is particularly apropos for this course because the course is much broader than its prominent philosophical and theological components.

Here, of course, we emphasize that this "worldview" is a Biblical one. And, the course designers also had a strong consensus among themselves that the general structure of the course should be on the historical principle rather on a topical one. This assumption lead to the question: What should be included in the course?

Assuming a Biblical perspective as all Christians ought to do, and assuming an historical approach, topics to be included became evident. First, it seemed obvious to start at the beginning and see what follows. For Christians the starting point or beginning is found in Genesis 1. There it says, "In the beginning God created the heavens and the earth." These words immediately implied some topics that ought to be included in the course. The word *beginning* suggests what philosophers call "cosmogony*,"* the question of origins. God, of course, is the focus of theology. *Created* is a sort of cognate of "cosmogony" because it refers to the origins of what God willed and planned and spoke into being. The phrase "the heavens and the earth" refers to the universe (cosmos) that God made and is discussed by philosophers as *cosmology*. A bit later in the creation narrative, Genesis describes the creation of man and his place in the universe. And, as soon as there were several image-bearing creatures—man—living together, human relationships (society) were inevitable. The Genesis account also tells how man was to live, how he <u>ought</u> to live, in the Garden—before God and with each other. These relationships are called *ethical* because they are measured and determined by what the Creator God desired and mandated. Thus, an ethical sense must be viewed as one means of communication between God and Man, thus also having an image-bearing quality.

Any reflection on the first sentence in Genesis and on what we have inferred from it implies a claim of knowledge—the field of epistemology in philosophy which entails the study of the sources, the nature and the goals of what we know. This opening verse of Genesis imparts knowledge about how the creation began. Reflection, an image-bearing ability too, on any knowledge raises questions about ways of knowing the certainty of what we know. Or, as we liked to ask students informally: "How do you know you know," or "How do you know what you know is true?" Such discussions over the years have been fascinating both for students and professors.

A reader might wonder what makes this course different from earlier courses in the Religion/Bible Department beyond taking an historical approach. A crucial difference was in the application of a new methodology—one developed by scholars who were fully committed to a Biblical view of learning, well versed in theology and philosophy, and themselves creative thinkers. These scholars were mainly in the Dutch Reformed tradition, working in the Netherlands, South Africa, and the United States. Their work is frequently referred to as Christian philosophy because it focused on many issues inherent in developing a Christian worldview. One of their unique contributions to Christian thought was the idea that all thought rests upon what they call *presuppositions*. Parenthetically, we note too that these thinkers also examined the history of philosophy from this perspective and therein contributed a breath-taking historical taxonomy (classification) of Western thought.

But, more on the function of presuppositions: They flow from one's basic assumptions and convictions, and may be viewed as "pre-theoretical" because they are so deeply rooted in the core of one's personality that they escape rational efforts to grasp and "prove" them. It's a truism that something is authoritative in everyone's life. That "something" functions as a starting point. Presuppositions are to our comprehensive thought-life as "axioms" are to certain mathematical studies. You cannot prove either axioms or presuppositions logically, but you need them to move forward in your thinking on the subject. Everyone has presuppositions, though they are not usually recognized without serious reflection on the thought process. Presuppositions could include reason, experience, intuition, an "ism," Allah, or any one of a thousand other things. The creators of the religion/philosophy course all agreed that their starting point, their authority, is the Creator God of Revelation, and that the Christian worldview they were creating should be based on and governed by it.

It's helpful to see the basis of this view in a Bible passage, cited earlier, II Cor. 10: 4 ff., which says that we should "cast down vain imaginations, and everything that exalts itself against the knowledge of God, and bring our thoughts captive and obedient to the will of Christ." Notice that there are two kinds of knowledge mentioned here; "**vain** imaginations"—ideas that are utterly in opposition to "the knowledge of God," and ideas that are "captive and obedient to the will of Christ." It's worth observing here, too, that the context of this passage is a Pauline comment on spiritual warfare, warfare in which all Christians are engaged. This, of course, implies a conflict between a Biblical view of the world and man-made views of the world. Ultimately, all man-made views are the same. They are all some version of the famous observation of the Greek thinker Protagoras (450 B. C.), when he said, "MAN is the measure of all things," a statement quoted by citizens in the humanist kingdom ever since, even today.

Here we list a few biblical presuppositions or assumptions that help us organize our thinking as Christians. First, God says who He is—the Creator (of all things, visible and invisible), Sustainer (preserves and governs all things through His Providence), and Redeemer (of those called according to His purpose). Second, God says who man is—an image-bearing creature (with ability to commune with God for His glory), the crown of creation (highest in the order of earthly creatures), fallen (but redeemable through faith in Christ's atonement), appointed to be fruitful and multiply (populate the earth). Third, God says that the earth is man's home over which he is to rule and have dominion. As an image-bearing creature, man can also imitate—though imperfectly—the creative quality of the Creator.

Embedded in the discussion of how the course was created were the main topics traced in the initial religion/philosophy course. In sum, the topics are: God, Man, Knowledge, Cosmology, Society, and Ethics. Each was traced historically through the main cultural phases of Western civilization. These phases include:

1.) Biblical and Classical worldviews;
2.) Medieval Synthesis of Christian and Classical worldviews;
3.) The Reformation worldview—Biblical Roots Recovered;
4.) Renaissance Humanism—in which many assumed that "man was the measure of all things";
5.) Enlightenment and Naturalistic worldviews (18th and 19th centuries) that assume Truth is obtained from a systematic study of the natural world without reference to any higher (transcendent) power; and,
6.) Modern worldviews—Positivism, Pragmatism, and Existentialism (19th and 20th century) worldviews, all on a humanistic foundation.

Pouring the six main course topics through the sieve of each worldview mentioned obviously presented a substantial intellectual challenge. Many professors who have taught this curriculum testify to the daunting nature of the task—both in the breadth of the subject matter and the effort required to present material at the undergraduate level. Yet, to a person, professors testified to the satisfaction in participating in this intellectual endeavor. Indeed, the course created the foundation of a solid education. That, we believe, has been the result of requiring this course of all Grove City College students since the early 1970s. Of course, this process has been enhanced by subsequent revisions and by other required courses in the Keystone Curriculum.

After more than a decade of teaching and refining this course, with the help of additional gifted faculty committed to the same Christian perspective, a two-volume collection of essays on it was published. W. Andrew Hoffecker was the principal editor of the collection, a publication entitled *Building a Christian World View*. It was published in two volumes (1986, 1988) by Presbyterian and Reformed Publishing, Phillipsburg, New Jersey.

Though this work is out of print, used copies are readily available on Amazon and in used bookstores. Yet, *Building a Christian World View* deserves to be reprinted as is; or better still, in a revised edition.

Summing up the impact of the religion/philosophy course on the spiritual life of the College during the MacKenzie era, it is fair to say that it was revolutionary. Why? Now students were equipped intellectually to understand the increasingly secular character of American society and apply a Biblical worldview to all areas of life, including their studies and future employment. Not only were students confronted with a robust presentation of the Biblical worldview, they also wrestled with prominent non-Christian thinkers. They learned the worldview of classical Greeks like Plato and Aristotle, the ideas of major Enlightenment philosophers Descartes, Locke, Hume and Kant and modern secular thinkers Marx, Freud and Crick. Students emerged from this two-semester course with an understanding of how thoughtful Christians can respond to Paul's challenge to "take captive" ideas that are opposed to the Biblical worldview.

From the point of view of this essay, we note that this course not only built on the Christ-centered view of the College's founders but constructed an **intellectual bridge** from their era to the modern secular world. In this the soul of the College was vastly strengthened. The record shows that many Grove City College graduates in the decades since have contributed to building solid marriages, families, and work-place spiritual/ethical climates that displayed their understanding of the tension between a Christian worldview and other spiritual systems.

One more important point is needed here. The religion/philosophy course did not remain stagnant once the MacKenzie era ended. Eventually, the structure changed from the use of a mass class meeting followed by smaller discussion sections to the more traditional formula of classes of about 35 students. No doubt this change made the course more effective. Further, new faculty were continually added, each with significant graduate studies. And, the topics of the course, while retained, were re-arranged, eventually leading to the pattern evident in the current College *Bulletin*. A perusal of this material will show that the primary principles on which this course was founded remain. Grove City College is probably the only school in the country that requires a series of core courses based on a mature understanding of what a Christian perspective means for the interface or harmonious bringing together of faith and learning. Such has been the effect of the religion/philosophy curriculum.

To what extent the perspectives and content of the other Keystone courses contributed to the improvement of the College's spiritual life is a question to ponder as we turn to an evaluation of them. We turn first to the Creative Keystone Curriculum.

B. The Creative Keystone Curriculum

Staffing the new Creative Keystone proved to be more problematic. MacKenzie took several faculty members from the English, Modern Language, and History departments to staff this course. Most of the faculty in these departments had been hired by President Harker in the wake of the loss of accreditation in 1956. During the first years of this course's operation, it became clear that most of the faculty were not trained in, or committed to, the idea of a Christian perspective in their fields. In fact, most were of the same mind as Dean of Men Fred Kring which we earlier characterized as secular humanism. It took some years before replacements for them by faculty with a Christian perspective were hired.

This course was initiated at the same time the religion/philosophy course was developed. Its structure and perspective were different from the religion/philosophy course, with the exception of a section or two taught by faculty who self-consciously held a Christian worldview. Naturally, they took up their teaching assignment from this perspective.

The purpose of this course, however, was to expose students to creative or artistic ways mankind had expressed itself through time. Principal forms of such expressions included art (painting), architecture, music, sculpture, and literature.

Though humanistically-oriented faculty evaluated artistic genre based on the presupposition that "Man is the measure of all things," they had their choice as to which <u>man</u> they would use as the measure at any particular time. They could use a man who was a contemporary of the artist or piece they were examining, or they could use another artist and piece from another era. A third option for a faculty member, often used, would be to evaluate (measure) the piece in question from his/her own perspectives—however "far out" they might be. Several faculty were classic "children of the '60s" with a "beatnik" or "existentialist" perspective. Such views were certainly distant from standard humanism, not to mention a Biblical perspective. They, of course, could all use the views found in a textbook also.

For some years each faculty member was free to make his/her own course outline. Some did not make any outline, until years later when the Dean required it for accreditation evaluation. Eventually, under the leadership of the chairman of the English Department, there was agreement on a number of themes and people who ought to be studied in all sections of the course. Another unique feature of this course for years was the practice of having student assistants help faculty members. These students graded papers and led discussion groups, and on occasion gave tests. Years later this practice was dropped due to concerns about the quality of instruction in some sections of the course.

The faculty members who worked from a Biblical perspective basically mirrored the worldview taught in the religion/philosophy course. They worked through the same cultural eras used in that course—euphemistically tagged "from the Greeks to the freaks." Much emphasis was placed on comparing humanistic expressions in the various arts with artistic expressions that were clearly Christian in these sections of the course. An obvious difference between humanistically-oriented faculty members and those who were self-consciously Christian in perspective was in their view of man. Instead of man saying who he was, as was the practice in a humanistic perspective, Christian-oriented faculty began by noting that man was who God said he was—an image-bearing crown of creation. Presuppositions implied in this perspective were essentially the same as those used in the religion/philosophy course. These characteristics were summarized in our discussion of the religion/philosophy course and may be consulted in that section of this essay—with one exception.

Since the name and purpose of this course seeks to account for human expressions that are imaginative and creative, an observation or two about that term will be helpful. In the West ancients did not have a word for creativity. For example, Plato somewhere in the *Republic* asks whether a painter <u>makes</u> something. His answer was "no" because in his view the painter merely imitates. Moreover, from the ancients to the Modern era the content of imaginative works of art were thought of as being "discovered" by the artist. This concept is, of course, a cousin of philosophical arguments on the question whether "laws of nature" known to man are created or discovered. Moreover, in the Christian West it is often assumed that "creativity" actually flowed from Divine inspiration and man's image-bearing nature.

Here we make a final observation on the ancient notion that "Man is the measure of all things." That concept became prominent in the late Renaissance era and more firmly entrenched in the age of the Enlightenment. And, continuous efforts have been made ever since to account for the creative impulse as originating somehow in the inner consciousness of man.

From a Christian perspective the source of this capacity must continue to be viewed and celebrated as an element in the image-bearing nature of man, though at times tainted by sin. This approach encourages students to critique art from a Christian perspective, yet at the same time causing them to stand in awe and wonder at what God's creatures can produce. Faculty rooted in the humanistic tradition, however, could adopt this view, but are more likely to see the source of creativity originating and somehow evolving in man's inner consciousness—beyond the capacity of reason to grasp. No matter, ultimately man's skills and insights are celebrated purely because they are inherent in man's created nature. The Humanist tradition, of course, has presuppositions too, but its practitioners tend not to self-consciously see them.

Obviously, only those sections of the Creative Dimension course taught from the perspective of a Christian worldview advanced the spiritual life of the College. Candor requires saying that the sections taught by the humanistically-oriented—either in the "far out" versions or the standard version—hindered the advancement of the College's spiritual life. That is to say, this perspective worked against efforts to improve the condition of the soul of the College. Of course, the humanistic tradition could not help but show students a large range of beauty in the art, architecture, music, and literature that is part of the Western tradition. And, why? It was part of God's gifts to artists notwithstanding their faith. That is to say, it was part of God's grace common among all men.

Eventually, by the end of the MacKenzie era (1991), the structure of this course was changing. Mass sections with student assistants were jettisoned in favor of more traditionally sized (30 students) classes. In addition, more faculty with a Christian background were hired, gradually replacing the bevy of humanistic faculty that had taught this course. Significantly, the new faculty had specialized training in topics covered in the Creative Dimension course, e.g., music, and art history. A principal change was to require a course that focused almost exclusively on literature while other courses focused on the rest of the arts. The current *Bulletin* describes these courses and their content, including a conscious effort to compare and contrast a Christian view of artistic expressions with other views.

C. The Social Science Keystone Course

The Social Science Keystone course began two years after the Religion/Philosophy and Creative Dimension programs. Essentially, the staffing problem, with an exception or two, in the social science course was the same as it was in the humanities program. Several new faculty were hired to help staff the Social Science Key, their presence adding to needed staff in sociology, psychology, and political science. While a number of these people were personally active Christians, they seemed to have no conception of a Christian perspective in their fields. Thus, when this program was instituted, the prospect of it contributing to the improvement of the health of the College's soul was dim. On the other hand, the winsome personal faith of most of the faculty in this course prevented a mood of hostility towards curricular change based on Christian assumptions.

This course structurally began with two sections that met twice a week and were team taught, faculty members taking turns lecturing. A third section was a weekly discussion group. After about five years, meeting times reverted to the traditional three times a week format, each section taught by one of the faculty that had team-taught the larger sections. Attempts were made to have a common syllabus, but each faculty member tended to spend more time on his area of graduate study. Years later, as reflected in the current *Bulletin,* the course was changed fundamentally in an attempt to bring a Christian perspective to each of the social sciences. In this new manifestation each social science department offered a "foundations" course which the *Bulletin* says "provide a strong Christian worldview." As part of the core program all students are now required to take one of the "foundations" courses in the social science area. This practice assumes that all students will become acquainted with how a social scientist operates from a Christian perspective.

Most traditional historians do not think of themselves as social scientists; rather they think of their studies as scholarship in the humanities arena. With this view, traditional historians provide a broad perspective on the human condition—much like traditional literature and philosophy courses do. Traditional historians compare and contrast eras and civilizations, though there is a sub-set in the field who focus on statistical studies of people.

D. (Natural) Science Keystone Course

As for the Keystone concept in the sciences, some faculty were familiar with the "science-religion" issue that had been prominent in American education for decades. Yet, it also took some time before additional faculty were hired who had thought through and even written on the question of the interface of science and Christian perspective in learning.

At the time the College was founded, America's intellectual community was involved in deep discussions about claims in the name of the scientific method in relation to the faith claims of traditional American higher education. For some, there was warfare between science and religion, to paraphrase the title of a book by

Cornell University's professor Andrew Dickson White, published in 1896. This view fed the popular press and even politics as represented by William Jennings in the Scopes Trial of 1925. Today this is called the "conflict theory," the notion held by some that there was an inevitable tension, if not conflict, between science claims and faith claims.

Interestingly, many colleges like Amherst and Grove City at that time did not teach an inevitable conflict between science and religion. In my studies and writing I have had opportunity to look at both of these colleges and have concluded that their professors taught something more akin to a "complexity theory," which states that it is possible to see harmony between science and religion.

Grove City College's faith and science issue in the curriculum has evolved, if we may use that word here, into the practice of offering several courses in the faith, science, and technology area. Presently students are required to take one course of three variations on these themes. The *Bulletin* says that in them students will be provided perspectives on the "basic presuppositions and underpinnings of science and Christian faith." Obviously, for some years the College has hired faculty equipped to deal with the question of the relationship between faith and the scientific method, a type of faculty it did not have as the 18-hour Keystone Curriculum was designed in the early 1970s. Later iterations of the course, represented by current practices, certainly contributed to a better spiritual life in the College.

E. Concluding Remarks on the Keystone Curriculum

There can be no question about the fact that the installation of the Keystone curriculum initiated an era of profound reforms in the College's intellectual life, altering its perspective on faith and learning. A keystone is, of course, one which supports all other stones in the arch. The Religion/Philosophy course came to function as the keystone for all the other courses in the College curriculum.

While President MacKenzie thought that these innovations could be accomplished in a few years—perhaps in 5 or 10 years, it took much longer. From the perspective of decades later, it is clear that early success in the initiation of the religion/philosophy course set the tone and paved the way for many additional curricular reforms that eventually installed a presupposition-based worldview as the foundation of the College's intellectual life. Any perusal of current College *Bulletins* and publicity materials about the College support this observation. We emphasize, too, that the Keystone curriculum was expanded and renamed under Vice President and then-President Jerry Combee.

There is, of course, always room for further development of this perspective on faith and learning in the curriculum. Significantly, the College offers a summer workshop for interested faculty on faith and learning based on the Christian worldview discussed here. In time, this workshop will deepen the faculty's understanding of how to teach from this perspective—this worldview.

As for the College's intellectual life, the changes made were not just as a knee-jerk return to the founders' views, a kind of reactionary exercise. To be sure, the basic Biblical principles of the founders were restored, but they were now expressed in the context of a 20th-century Christian philosophy. This was a dramatic innovation.

It was not an effort to make Grove City College into a "Bible college" as some opponents of these changes had alleged. It represented, on the contrary, a conscious effort to get students to think Biblically, vigorously, and deeply about the subject matter covered in each course—an academic exercise was, and is therein, assured.

The challenge to "clean up student behavior," to improve ethical practices among students, took some time. Eventually a much larger number of self-confessing Christian students precipitated a spiritual revival. How that happened is the subject of the next chapter.

Chapter 6
Meeting the Challenge of Student Social Life in the MacKenzie Era

Introduction

In this chapter we consider the second part of J. Howard Pew's challenge to Charles MacKenzie, "Clean up student social life!" Efforts by President MacKenzie to clean up student life took a long time, continuing even after he retired in 1991. To be sure, solid achievements occurred along the way, but several crucial ones did not emerge until the early 1990s. We will consider the cleanup process in two parts. One will outline the scope and length of the party-school climate among students, building on Kring-era practices. A second section will rehearse administrative efforts to eradicate the party-school climate.

On reflection, it appears that new President MacKenzie faced a steep learning curve when it came to dealing with college students. He had recently turned 46 and married only a few years earlier. Thus, he had no personal experience in raising children or parenting young adults. In addition, he had spent the previous 15 years as a pastor in large Presbyterian churches. By all reports he was a very good preacher and an effective pastoral counselor. This did not prepare him, however, for dealing with rambunctious, party-minded 20-year-old students. He needed help. Before turning to reform efforts during his watch, we will flesh out the dimensions of student life that needed to be cleaned up.

A. Student Behavior During the 70s and 80s

We noted in Chapter 4 how student social life was managed by Dean Kring. Under his leadership, with President Harker's acquiescence or concurrence, a robust "party-school" atmosphere emerged. It was characterized by a two-nights-a-week party schedule—Wednesdays and Fridays. As we shall see later, it took a long time to instill a strong Christian flavor in student social life. If we cataloged fully the length and scope of student social practices during the Harker and MacKenzie years, it would take several books. Instead, we will create a montage that paints an accurate, though briefer picture, of party-life during these years. While not necessarily in an exact chronological order, the following practices, begun during the Kring years, characterized the MacKenzie years as well.

Dean Kring continued in office during MacKenzie's first two years; his support of the existing student practices continued as well. MacKenzie came to realize that he needed to replace Dean Kring. He re-assigned Kring to the Psychology Department faculty. MacKenzie had also made it clear that he intended to create a Christian atmosphere across the whole campus, department by department and dorm by dorm. He tells us in his "Reminiscence" that he was not prepared for the reaction that followed. It welled up among faculty and students as well as among some in the administration.

As for Professor Kring, he continued to spend much time "advising" students and socializing with the Harker-hired faculty, whom he had befriended during his years as Dean of Students. They joined him in dissenting from MacKenzie's efforts to bring Christian values to campus society. Together Kring and his faculty friends continued to encourage the radical Greek lifestyle of the fraternities and sororities. Kring invited his fraternity friends to his "farm" on the edge of town once it was in operation. They were, of course, free to party there anyway they wished.

The point here is, as we recount student behavior in the MacKenzie era, student dissent from MacKenzie's new policies was encouraged by faculty associated with Dean Kring. As noted before, Kring and his faculty friends were secular-minded people who embraced humanistic values rather than Christian ones.

Turning more specifically to student life in the MacKenzie era, we emphasize that it centered on fraternity life—and on sorority life to a lesser degree. As might be expected, the men set the tone for party life and the women joined, often by invitation. To be sure, the women had their own drinking habits as noted in Chapter 4 of this essay—rum in coke on the lawn, for example.

Most of the time there were 11 active fraternities on campus during these years, though all of them at one time or another lost their Charters due to a rules violation. Some of them lost their Charters for as many as four years. All of them were on probation at one time or another. Often while on probation, or without a charter, fraternities continued to act like fraternities without outward evidence of this practice—not wearing colors, for example. That is to say, they operated in an "underground" fashion.

Life in off-campus male housing seemed to grow more problematic during the early MacKenzie years. Though not permitted by school rules, many off-campus houses were, in effect, fraternity houses with a lifestyle that would even be envied by students from public universities. Often there seemed to be no limit on the range of activities that would take place in these houses.

Objectively speaking, this should be no surprise because Grove City College students were, on average, superior in ability and creative skills than most other college students in the nation.

If one were in a house next door to one of the "frat houses" on a Wednesday or Friday night, what could you expect to see and hear? Beer drinking would begin early and last until late into the night. Usually Sam Adams was joined by Jim Beam and some of his Kentucky friends, who together were in a mood for Southern Comfort. Likely there would be no discrimination against those present who were "underage." Frequently non-members might arrive with a member, or simply arrive uninvited. Most of them were welcomed—especially as joviality increased in proportion to the amount of beer consumed. Eventually, an observer would begin to smell pot along with much cigarette smoke. Off to one side it would be likely that various drugs were being consumed as well. Eventually music would become very loud. In time, the place would be packed with dancing couples, spilling out onto the porch or even onto the roof of the porch. Beer cans emptied outdoors found their way into neighboring yards as well. It must be said that sobered "brothers" in the morning hurried to pick up the cans. On numerous occasions neighbors called the College complaining about student reveling, often calling Dean of Students Ross Foster at all hours of the night.

Many veterans of these party years also note that some fraternity houses were located to the north of the campus while others were on the south side. The point is that on party nights there would be hundreds of students trekking back and forth across the campus, usually raucously, from parties on one side to the other.

An important part of fraternity life was selecting and accepting new members. Many of the events associated with this process were imaginative and displayed great talent. A decidedly down-side to the initiation process was the hazing of the pledges. Hazing included rituals involving harassment, abuse, and humiliation which often resulted in physical or psychological pain. It seems that the scope of hazing was limited only by the imagination of its practitioners. Particularly sad hazing incidents occurred several times when "well-greased" pledges were blindfolded and driven out into the country and dropped off with directions to find their way home. Most pledges were, of course, from some other areas and did not know where they were. While marching back along rural roads, on two occasions pledges were run down by drunk drivers approaching from the rear. Several died from massive injuries. These events were very sobering for the College community. Subsequently, new rules prohibited such marches.

To brighten the story here a bit, we note a hazing event from the 1990s which shows the impact of administrative reforms by that time. Instead of traditional physical hazing, a newly re-constituted fraternity (after the loss of a charter) announced a public event in which the brothers of this fraternity washed the feet of the brothers of a rival fraternity. Apparently Jesus had visited them.

Another positive example of fraternity practices should include the habit of brothers helping others in their fraternities who were weak in a certain course. Tutoring and studying together were typical practices—no doubt an example of brotherly love.

We make two more points in this composite account of student life—largely fraternity life. One, not all students were involved, in the kind of party life described here. This raises the question of how many students from the 70s to the 90s were self-identified Christians. Anecdotal evidence from students and from Student Affairs officials from that era suggests that it would be about 10 percent of the students. Many other students were nominal Christians who left their tenuous commitment at home when they came to college. Still others had no outward appearance of Christian values or commitment.

Another point needs to be made as we conclude this picture of student behavior in the MacKenzie era. Some fraternities had members who were active in varsity sports. In some cases it was the habit of fraternity brothers to use speed while playing in these sports. One freshman student at the time tells a story about the first day he arrived in the locker room to begin practice. It was customary for the College to provide new and then clean clothes to the athletes. As he began to put on his socks, he noticed that there was something in the toe. Reaching in the sock, his hand came out full of assorted pills. His response was, in a loud voice, "Hey, guys what are these for?" A senior immediately shushed him up and said in a quiet voice, "Those are energy pills—speed. They make you play better and faster." Apparently this was a common practice in some locker rooms.

We conclude this section on student behavior with a question we have asked before: How did student behavior, especially in fraternities, enhance the spiritual life of the College? What did it do for the life of the College's soul? The answer is clear and brief. Rather than improve the spiritual climate and strengthen the soul of the College, the rather riotous living of students diluted the power and influence of the College's spirituality. As for the soul, it was wounded: Perhaps, even made sick unto death. Could the roots of the College's spiritual life recover?

We turn now to a consideration of administrative efforts that eventually lead to a recovery of a spiritual climate that honored the traditions and practices of the founders. This recovery of Christian values among students is remarkable, if not unique, even among contemporary Christian colleges.

B. Reforming Student Behavior: The 70s to the 90s

Our main focus here is on efforts to "clean up" student behavior which began in 1973 with the appointment of Ross Foster as Dean of Students. There were, however, several related developments that preceded his appointment and on reflection seem to have been a special Providence in the renewal of the College's spiritual life.

1. Some Preliminary Matters

One of these was the arrival on the campus of several freshmen students who came from homes and churches that were solidly Reformed (old style) in their theology. They soon began their own Bible study which read widely on contemporary Reformed theology. Terry Thomas '74 was the leader of this group and was taking a class from philosophy professor Ross Foster (not yet appointed Dean of Students). Foster was teaching from a new Reformed perspective that was dominated by an apologetic developed among Dutch thinkers, a view he learned in his seminary training. Thomas was enamored by this perspective and asked Foster to speak to his student group about it. Thomas' group was a remnant of the decades-old Campus Christian Union.

When Foster came to speak about eight students were present. This most popular professor asked about its membership. He was informed that membership was about 30 students, but only a few came to each meeting. Foster, surprised at the low number, thought it was remarkable that only about 30 students were involved in the only Christian student group on campus out of a student body of about 1,800 students. Foster—a superb teacher—met regularly with these students and began to unfold the scope of a Christian worldview and how one ought to live in the world as a Biblical Christian.

Another remarkable event occurred at about the same time. The Thomas group decided to read a little book entitled *Escape from Reason* (1968) by Francis Schaeffer, an internationally acclaimed Christian thinker. Thomas says "the book blew me away" because it was such a powerful defense of a Christian worldview, with its emphasis on the necessity of beginning with a recognition of one's presuppositions. Another student asked, "Why don't we ask Schaeffer to come and speak to us?" "He lives in Switzerland," someone replied. "Write him anyway," was yet another comment. A letter was sent, inviting him to come and speak. In days a reply came in which Schaefer said he would be delighted to come. He added, "My first church as a pastor was Covenant Church in Grove City and I would love to see it again."

Weeks later he arrived and spoke to a packed fieldhouse, strikingly dressed in his Swiss lederhosen. He laid out the basic ideas of a Biblical perspective—a foreign language, no doubt, to most of the students present. At the end of the lecture he took questions. At one point, a tall blond man stood up and asked a question in a booming voice. Thomas thought that only the questioner and Schaeffer understood the question. He whispered to his friends, "We need to find out who that guy is. He thinks just like Schaeffer!" After the lecture, they introduced themselves to "that man" and it turned out to be Professor Pete Steen of Geneva College. Thus began a long friendship.

Steen left Geneva at the end of that school year and moved to Grove City to begin a new career as an itinerant professor of philosophy who lectured regularly on a dozen campuses in Western Pennsylvania, also spending much time in informal gatherings of students. Steen's principal sponsor was the CEO of Archer, Daniels, Midland Corporation. His message was the same as Ross Foster's and Francis Schaeffer's—one had to **think** about the world from the point of view of his presuppositions. Thomas and his friends spent much time with Professor Steen during the next years.

A remarkable feature of these events was the fact that Foster, Schaeffer, and Steen all had read and studied the same materials in their seminary training. Schaeffer and Steen were both trained in Westminster Seminary in Philadelphia---Schaeffer a generation before Steen. Interestingly, Foster was trained in the Reformed Episcopal Seminary in Philadelphia, which was a mirror image of Westminster, except that its faculty thought an Episcopal church structure was preferable to a Presbyterian one.

In addition to spending much time with Grove City College students, Steen also became friends with the new faculty members MacKenzie hired to create the Religion/Philosophy course, faculty who were also trained in the same presuppositional tradition.

Within months after the Thomas-Schaeffer-Steen encounter, Charles MacKenzie arrived and began his efforts to reform student behavior. Looking back, it seems like the Thomas-Schaeffer-Steen nexus was a Special Providence because it planted a seed which flowered to support Ross Foster when MacKenzie appointed him Dean of Students months later. Moreover, the Thomas group not only continued to study with Ross Foster during their last two years as students; they also studied with the new Religion/Philosophy faculty after they arrived.

One more exceptional circumstance fed the MacKenzie reform effort just as it began—the initial meeting of Professor Foster and newly arrived Professor Van Til. The 1972 school year began with an opening faculty worship service run by the Religion Department. Each member took part in the service. Foster's task that night was to pray. When he finished, Van Til said to his wife, "That man is in the Reformed Tradition." Afterward, as was customary, some faculty gathered for a dessert in the home of the Assistant Dean of Men. The Fosters arrived a bit late and immediately were met with a rousing razzing about the length of his prayer. It was much too long for the taste of many. Obviously, this was not the first time that Foster was treated this way.

It was here that the Fosters and Van Tils met. It did not take long for them to realize that each was a devotee of the presuppositional worldview. A week later the Van Tils were invited to the Fosters for a Saturday evening dinner. Thereafter, they were friends, allies, and active intellectual companions, working for decades to help reform Grove City College's intellectual life and student behavior.

Only days before this encounter, Van Til had met Professor Hoffecker as they both moved into offices on the top floor of Crawford Hall. The result was the same as it had been at the meeting of Foster and Van Til.

Hoffecker and Van Til recognized that they, too, were cut from the same cloth. It was not long before these three began to design the Religion/Philosophy course, as noted earlier.

2. Beginning the Reform of Student Behavior

We noted already that within a year of taking office President MacKenzie realized that Dean Kring's philosophy was diametrically opposed to his and dissented from the College's Christian foundations. The result was the reassignment of Kring to the faculty. This left MacKenzie with the question of who should replace him as Dean of Students. At the suggestion of several of his new faculty hired to create the Rel/Phil course, he interviewed and then hired Ross Foster. This marked a decisive turning point in the operation of the Dean of Students office, soon renamed Student Affairs. It would be a long time, however, before the student party-lifestyle would be turned around.

Foster, like MacKenzie, was an ordained Presbyterian minister, though a half-generation younger and with a family. He also had graduate studies in philosophy. His worldview was in the Reformed tradition like the founders of the College and J. Howard Pew's. Once appointed Dean of Students, he continued to help teach and develop the Religion/Philosophy course. Eventually it was in this course that he found numerous, deeply committed Christian students who he would hire to fill the Resident Assistant positions in the dorms, including Terry Thomas discussed above. When he arrived in the Student Affairs office to take up his new duties, he was met with a number of interesting conditions. First was the fact that out-going Dean Kring's assistant remained—a person who had Kring's perspective on life at that time. The Dean of Women was a polite, older unmarried woman whose outlook would be closer to remnants of the dying Victorian culture that still haunted the town.

Management of Student Affairs included the employment of Resident Directors who were responsible for a whole dorm or large section of a sizable dorm. They were helped by students employed as Resident Assistants, usually responsible for one floor of students.

C. Changes that Made up the Backbone of Student Behavioral Reforms

Before enumerating reform efforts, we need to state clearly again what needed to be reformed. By the end of the Harker/Kring era two main qualities characterized the student body. First, only about 10 percent were actively Christian. Other students came from nominally Christian homes but appeared to have left their tenuous Christian faith at home before matriculating at Grove City College. Second, by the time President MacKenzie arrived in late 1971, the rhythm of student life was dominated by drinking, drugs, and other forms of corrupted virtue—lead by an increasingly active off-campus fraternity life. These two factors were intimately linked. Thus, both needed to be the focus of reform as the process began.

Much research and reflection suggested that it took most of 25 years after the arrival of MacKenzie to achieve the goal of reconstituting student life. Or, in the language of J. Howard Pew, it took 25 years to "clean up student behavior."

Hundreds of factors went into this long process—enough material for a book all by itself. We can, however, distill all of this down to a manageable number of people and events that made up the backbone of student behavioral reforms. We will list them and then discuss each—some in more detail than others:

> 1. The appointment of Ross Foster as Dean of Students;
> 2. Foster's immediate decision to select RAs **himself**;
> 3. The arrival of CCO (Coalition for Christian Outreach) to help staff Student Affairs. This was a Pittsburgh-based group who sought to have a Young-Life-type experience for children in the region's colleges;
> 4. Hiring of self-consciously Christian faculty;
> 5. Closing of off-campus housing in 1982;
> 6. A campaign to enroll Christian students;
> 7. A gradual shift in chapel programming.

This discussion of the main threads that made up reforms in Student Affairs will be followed by another Chapter that will add a miscellany of topics. Items there may strike the reader as funny, sad, shocking, surprising, scary, or just plain sophomoric stupidity. In this way a bit more color will be added to the reform efforts that certainly were sober at times.

1. The Appointment of Ross Foster as Dean of Students

Others writing about the College during the MacKenzie years say virtually nothing about Foster's role in Student Affairs. This essay has made scattered comments about his background, training, and popularity as a teacher soon after he arrived, including his actual appointment as Dean of Students in 1973. He held this position, which was eventually retitled Vice President for Student Affairs, for 17 years. More than anyone else he was responsible for initiating and carrying forward changes that improved the Christian character of student life on the campus. Though a brilliant logician, warm, friendly, and humorous, Ross Foster possessed real wisdom in decision-making. On the other hand, Foster was self-effacing, perhaps to a fault. Some who are familiar with the College over several decades insist that he was the most effective and fair-minded administrator the institution has had in modern times. His role will be obvious in the discussion that follows.

2. Dean Foster's Decision to Immediately Hire RAs Himself

Much of the improvement in student behavior over the decades being examined here was due to the steady increase in the number of active Christian students on campus. One administrative change that contributed to this development was the hiring of Christian RAs. Before Foster began his tenure in Student Affairs in 1973, it had been customary for decades for departing RAs to select their own replacements. Most of the time this meant that one fraternity brother would select an RA from his fraternity to take his place. This practice continued the fraternity-party lifestyle in the dorms for years. Indeed, this practice made it difficult to break party patterns among the students.

Foster decided to select new RAs himself by way of an interview which included a question whether the RA candidate would be willing to pray with a troubled Freshman. This, of course, drove away candidates who had no personal prayer life. Two things followed. One, word went out among fraternities that they should not apply for RA positions any more. Two, word circulated among Christian students that these jobs were available to them, assuming that they qualified in all other ways.

Fraternity brothers thought this process was unfair, even complaining to President MacKenzie, who complained to Foster. Since Foster saw this as an important step in reining in party life, he said he intended to continue the practice. If President MacKenzie insisted on a return to the previous policy, Foster offered to resign—this being one of nine times he offered to resign over policy matters during his 17 years in Student Affairs. Foster continued as Dean of Students.

3. The Arrival of CCO to Help Staff Student Affairs

Many Pittsburgh area high schools had benefited from the presence of Young Life programs on their campuses for several decades by 1970. Business leaders and clergy in the area recognized that Young Life's Biblical perspective on life was severely challenged when the students went off to college. They resolved to build an organization that would be available to their students once they arrived on college campuses. The result in 1970 was the incorporation of the Coalition for Christian Outreach (CCO). It soon was staffed with people able to train Christian college graduates to go back on campus to tell students about the "claims of Christ on their lives." CCO workers took jobs in area colleges, often in the student affairs departments. From there they would reach out and train student leaders who, in turn, organized Bible studies and many other student activities. A signal feature of CCO people was their ability to spend time relating on a one-on-one basis with students, especially those who were homesick, or just overwhelmed by college life.

A particularly interesting feature of CCO programs, past and present, is that they clearly have a Biblical perspective, that is, worldview. And, why? An early teacher of CCO student trainees before they went off to campuses to work was none other than Pete Steen. He was joined by Terry Thomas, Jim Thrasher (who later was very successful leading the College's Career Services Office), and other like-minded people once they finished college. Many of them stayed with CCO for years, even decades. In this regard, Andrew Hoffecker, who helped frame the original Keystone course, also taught biblical worldview at staff training sessions in the 1980s which were held at Penn State University, Kent State University and Geneva College. These coincidences illustrate that material which helped shape the soul of Grove City College also filtered out into Christian ministries to colleges in other parts of the country.

Parenthetically, readers should google CCO and look at the range of services they offer. One more point here, and a stunning one: CCO has grown to the point that, at this writing, it has missions on over 115 campuses. The original vision was to serve colleges in Western Pennsylvania. Now, it serves colleges from Indiana in the West to Yale in the East.

In this context, it is easier to see that when CCO came to Grove City College, it aided in the development of a Christian perspective among students on the Grove City College campus. To emphasize the significance of CCO staff members on the campus, we note some of the areas in which they worked. Many of them were Head Residents (Resident Directors) and in this position were able to help select and guide student Resident Advisors, demonstrating how to operate Bible studies and other wholesome activities. Other CCO staff were assistant coaches or deeply involved in intramural sports. We here mention some staff members because some readers of this essay may have been on campus when they were there. Mention of them also serves to honor their contributions towards improving student behavior during Ross Foster's years in Student Affairs: Terry Thomas, Tom McWhertor, David (Ph.D.) and Cynthia Guthrie, John (Ph.D.) and Nancy Currid, Ridge and Connie Orr, and John Trushel. Rev. Joe McDonald seems to have been the first CCO person hired by Grove City College, serving as College Chaplain for a short time. CCO's influence on the Grove City campus can be seen from the fact that from 1970 to the present, over 50 CCO staff have served on the campus. A final note: CCO workers had to raise a significant amount of money for their own financial support, the College contributing the rest.

4. Hiring Dedicated Christian Faculty

MacKenzie worked hard to hire faculty who could think Biblically, and thus, help change the structure and content of the curriculum. An important side-effect of this process was the impact these people had on the Christian student movement. Many of these new faculty were able to show students how to integrate faith and learning, and how to critique the continuing humanistic influence among the older faculty. Others were disposed to hold Bible studies in their homes for students, some continuing this practice for several decades. Still others spoke to student groups, including new ones that emerged, such as the Salt Company. The impact of this contingent of new faculty on improving student behavior should not be under estimated. In a few words, many new Christian faculty hired by MacKenzie had a double-barreled effect on students—socially and intellectually. The soul of Grove City College was healthier due to their efforts.

One of President MacKenzie's early hires, John Sparks, deserves special mention here. Sparks has had much influence on the development of a Christian atmosphere and a Christian perspective on faith and learning in the College. He was Man of the Year while a student at the College. After graduating from the University of Michigan's School of Law, he taught in Hillsdale College for several years, and then returned to his Alma Mater to teach. During his tenure at the College, Sparks taught in and chaired the Department of Business, taught in the core program, anchored the Constitutional Law program, and served many years as Dean of the Calderwood School of Arts and Letters. His effect on the development of the College was much greater than merely working in these positions might suggest.

Sparks' Christian wisdom was much sought after by students, other faculty, and the College's administrators. But, John Sparks' gifts and wisdom did not arrive with him when he matriculated at the College. He was fond of speaking in the Chapel every few years and telling how he became a Christian and what it meant in his life. In sum, the story is as follows. While at the College and active in a fraternity and in student government, he met Marion Malarkey. Marion herself earlier became a Christian through the efforts of her Young-Life-trained brothers. She married John and they went off to Michigan Law School. While there, they talked about Christianity regularly. Part of John's late evening reading included plowing through a complex theological book entitled *Defense of the Faith*. At some point he recognized his need to commit to the claims of Christ, which he soon did. Everyone who knows John Sparks knows that he is a stellar Christian in all facets of his life. Much more could be said, but one more item needs to be noted. Sparks has taught by word and by deed many on the faculty, in the administration, and on the College's Board what Christian faith means for the life of the College. In this he has defended and advanced the quality of the life of the College's soul.

5. Closing of Off-Campus Housing in 1982

Some headway in improving student behavior was made in the dorms during the first decade of President MacKenzie's tenure, thanks to efforts by Dean Foster and a number of dedicated CCO staff. At the same time, some off-campus housing morphed into fraternity housing. The party lifestyle from the Kring days intensified.

Attempts to "police" frat activity were not easy. Even fines for drinking violations, suspension for second and third violations, and dismissal of some from the College did not have a substantial effect on improving behavior. These were, after all, talented, imaginative Grover students, who could find ways to circumvent the rules. Moreover, while partying continued in the defacto frat houses, there was a tendency to hold parties some distance from the campus on a regular basis. These would take place at rented facilities in towns as much as 30 miles away.

One former Dean of Men tells, what appears to be a typical story, about how such parties were conducted. The way he learned about this particular party is interesting too. Suspicious of intelligence that a big party had been held in another town at a large hall, he called the manager of the hall and told him that he was Dean of Men at Grove City College and wanted to know how the students who rented the hall had behaved. Apparently unaware that such parties were against school rules, the manager enthusiastically told the Dean of Men all about the boys and their party. They sent over their payment in advance, arrived early to decorate the premises on party day, wheeled in their kegs of beer, and brought in a band by party time. They behaved very well, the manager said, much better than students from a neighboring college six miles to the south of Grove City. When finished, the manager continued, they cleaned up the hall better than his own help would do. And, the boys thanked him on the way out. They were welcome to the hall anytime, he told the Dean.

    The Dean looked into the matter. One difficulty was the fact that some of the brothers and their female companions were underage drinkers. This condition was a violation of civil law and thus subjected the students to discipline by the College. Ending such party practices was not easy because they usually were secretive events. A big concern of this Dean was the safety of the students travelling to and from such parties, likely in an intoxicated condition.

    Parties continued in town during these years too. Two factors continued to be causal, according to Dean Foster. One was the continued absence of a substantial Christian influence in the fraternities. The other factor was the difficulty in monitoring fraternity life in the defacto fraternity houses. Off-campus defacto fraternity life ended in a surprising way. The inter-fraternity council wrote the Chairman of the Board and complained that the disciplining of fraternities for violations was uneven. The Board considered the matter for a time and concluded that the only way to end this was to close all off-campus housing. In 1981 it announced that 1981-82 would be the last year for off-campus housing.

One result, of course, was a sharp drop in student parties. One imaginative fraternity eventually had its graduate older brothers buy a dwelling under a corporate name and then make it available for fraternity use, "as a study center," they said. The closing of the defacto fraternity houses pushed some of the parties back onto the campus. For some time the Student Affairs Office was busy tracking down stashes of beer, booze, and pot in dorm rooms.

Dean Foster has recounted how this process resulted in a collection of confiscated bongs in his office that numbered more than 30 at one point. He liked to point out how—he had a sense of humor—creative students were able to retrieve some of these bongs. While he was out of his office and his young helper was busied by students in conversation, a fraternity brother snuck into his office and took a bong or two. He knew this because after a week or so he realized that the bong count had dropped. Thereafter, he locked his door. The bongs were, of course, evidence in matters of discipline.

Even though off-campus fraternity housing was at times problematic during the first decade of MacKenzie's tenure, overall conditions improved. This improvement was due to imaginative efforts by Dean Foster and by the steady, but slow, growth of the number of Christian students on campus. The work of CCO staff was also most helpful.

By the time off-campus housing was shut down, Dean Foster tells us that in his view a full "cleanup of student behavior" would only work if a concerted effort was made to enroll large numbers of Christian students. That move would be made soon.

6. A Campaign to Enroll Christian Students

Foster made his views on the need for Christian students known to MacKenzie. MacKenzie listened but wondered how this could be accomplished. Foster suggested that the College's admissions literature sent out to high school students could be more explicit on its Christian principles. MacKenzie was concerned about the cost. Foster also suggested that the hundreds of Christian schools, and Christian home-schooled students could be directly contacted. Another concern of MacKenzie was the fact that the College already had a high rate of applicants for each opening.

After some investigation, and Foster had learned to be a good sleuth as Dean of Students, he told the President that the current admissions program was tilted in favor of accepting fraternity and sorority candidates. This was especially the case, he said, when a parent of such candidates had graduated from the College. The side-effect of this process was that fewer active Christian applicants were offered admission to the College. After several years of hearing this argument from Foster, MacKenzie agreed to consider changes in the admissions program. Vice President Jerry Combee supported the idea as well. In fact, Combee had a candidate in mind to head up the Admissions Department, Jeff Mincey.

Mincey took office in 1990 and stayed through 2011. The hallmark of his program was the fact that he personally read every student essay included in the application. Part of this essay had to comment on the student's religious affiliation in view of the College's mission. Mincey saw it as natural to give preference to obviously Christian students—everything else being equal. Mincey also gradually changed the admissions staffing—especially the part-time student escorts who showed candidates around the campus. In addition, Mincey hired recent graduates with strong Christian credentials to work as interviewers, sifting for good candidates.

What was the result of Mincey's program? Almost immediately many admissions materials were changed to reflect a Christian emphasis. Moreover, many faculty soon reported that they could feel a new spirit among many students. Student Affairs reported a gradual drop in rule violations.

Interviews with students from the mid-1990s and administrators who worked in the College at that time suggest that by 1995 the College had reached a new stage. Not only were academics more tuned to a Christian perspective, and at the same time, more demanding, student behavior was now presumed to meet Christian standards. In other words, student behavior had been cleaned up. What J. Howard Pew requested of Charles MacKenzie, "Clean up student behavior," had been largely achieved. From another angle, the soul of Grove City College was more attuned to the spirit of the founders than it had been for decades.

As a concluding point here, we note that by this time people tended to refer to Grove City College as a "Christian College" rather than as a "Church-related College," as it had been for decades. This, too, is evidence of the changes that have been described here.

7. A Gradual Shift in Chapel Programs

Attending chapel exercises had always been part of student life in Grove City College. We outlined this in some detail in the beginning of this essay. By the last decade of the Weir Ketler era (1940s), chapel had settled down into a five-day-a-week *proforma* routine which consisted of announcements, a hymn, a reading of a few verses from the Bible without comment, a prayer, and a singing of the Alma Mater. Apparently this continued for years after Stanley Harker became President.

One of the first things Harker did was to change the chapel program. He ended Saturday sessions because, he said, it interfered with football games and other social events. He also ended segregation of students in chapel exercises by sex—males on one side and females on the other. A new method of taking role in Chapel was possible too. Students now turned in IBM cards. Chapel continued to be conducted according to the same format described above. Still, these changes brought the worship format into the 20th century.

Yet, we may conclude that chapel exercises were not particularly edifying. That is to say, from the point of view of this essay, the soul of the College during these decades was probably at risk of needing life-support, or so some Christian students of the Harker years have opined.

The office of College Pastor went through several stages over the years. For decades a senior member of the Bible Department held this post. He seemed to have no special duties except to assign faculty to read Scripture and pray. Near the end of the Harker era, J. Howard Pew hired a pastor without consulting Harker, a point mentioned in an early part of this essay. Harker did not re-hire him, but appointed a young seminary graduate and named him College Chaplain. His duties were expanded to include counseling students. Apparently, he did more than counsel several female students. Later, his divorced wife made a point of bringing this information to members of the Bible (now named "Religion") Department, stating that this was the reason she divorced him and moved to another state.

Soon, yet another young pastor was hired by the newly-installed President MacKenzie to be College Chaplain. It became clear immediately, however, that he was not equipped by education or experience to conduct meaningful chapel exercises.

He was replaced by an experienced Presbyterian preacher who was well known for his speaking ability. His name was Bruce Thielemann. He was an imposing and entertaining person in many ways. And, he insisted on a more elevated title for his new job. He was now "Dean of the Chapel" and paid a handsome salary. Possessed with a silver tongue, he was a master rhetorician. Thus, he was able to make his audience laugh one moment, only to make them cry the next. His theology was geared to make listeners feel that he was speaking to their tradition. He also referred frequently to his own demons. For example, he tipped the scale at over 300 pounds and often talked about his struggle with food, eliciting sympathy from his audience. This struggle caused marriage to elude him, he said. Loneliness was the result.

Most everyone who heard Bruce Thielemann preach was moved in his spirit. In a few words, Thielemann was a brilliant orator. He served in this post for 11 years and then took a call to pastor Pittsburgh's famous First Presbyterian Church. Thielemann certainly brought more dignity and excitement to Chapel exercises. In this he stirred the soul of the College.

Rev. Richard Morledge, pastor of the Bakerstown Presbyterian Church, located 40 miles southeast of Grove City, was hired as a part-time College pastor to take the place of Rev. Thielemann. He commuted between his church and the College for years. This Grover served for more than a decade and a half in the post, having a special affection for the school as a graduate. Like Thielemann, he held several honorary degrees in theology.

Being single, too, he was able to spend much time with students and was much loved and respected. He created numerous programs that involved students in service programs in the region. During his tenure the spiritual life of students improved substantially, that is to say, the soul of the College was further stirred to action by his Biblically-based messages and programs.

Morledge was followed in 1999 by the Rev. Stanley Keehlwetter, who continues to serve as Dean of the Chapel, working as well as an instructor in the humanities program. His education and pastoral experience has been in the Evangelical tradition. Rev. Keehlwetter holds an earned doctorate from Fuller Seminary.

Since this essay is not intended to evaluate the spiritual life of the College during the most recent years—that would be a journalistic account rather than an historical one—we make only one comment on the current Chapel program. There is no doubt about the fact that during the past decade and a half there have been many innovations that have helped broaden student involvement in spirit-driven matters. In short, the program has fed the souls of students, and thus, most importantly, the soul of the College has been noticeably enlivened.

Chapter 7
An Assemblage of Miscellaneous Stories Touching Student Affairs

In the previous chapters we characterized the problem of wayward students, stated administrative goals for changing their behavior, discussed a number of people and programs that were central to the process, and emphasized that a main factor in improving student behavior was an active program to recruit more Christian students. This process took much longer than expected: Most of a generation (1971-1995). Our account of all this is brief to be sure. Yet, its significance is best understood as a chapter in the full history of the spiritual life of the College—from the days of Isaac Ketler to the present hour. In that context, these 25 years was a time that tried the soul of the College, just like the souls of many other colleges with a Christian label. Unlike many church-related colleges that effectively marginalized or outright rejected their original Christian foundation in the 20th century, Grove City College is unique in that efforts to save and regenerate the soul of the College have prevailed.

Scattered through this recovery process are many additional striking events and people that were not injected into the narrative. It seemed like a good idea to include some of them here, near the end of this narrative though they occurred much earlier, to add some color and stimulate further thinking about the development of the College. Each is interesting and informative. Some are sad and sobering; others, humorous; still others are perhaps even shocking. These stories are not presented in any particular chronological order.

One more point: Our interest here is the effect the following people and events had on the soul of the College, not to single out individuals for public identification. Thus, names are infrequently mentioned.

* * * *

Soon after he arrived, Ross Foster began to hear stories about various aberrant spiritual practices on campus from students in his World Religions class. Following inquiries, he learned that for years a professor had been active in the Church of Ageless Wisdom, a form of Devil worship. Foster sought him out and asked about the matter. At first the professor was reluctant to talk. Foster invited him to speak in his World Religions class, and the professor was still reluctant. Foster assured him that he had academic freedom to say whatever he wished. A week later the professor appeared and began to lay out the nature of his spiritual views. From time to time, Foster had to re-assure him of his academic freedom. Some of his presentations included the following information. It was clear that he had been active in town for years, even having had a convention of like-minded worshipers in Carnegie Hall. He also had a number of followers among female students who met on their own in covens in their dorms. Frequently on Sunday evening after chapel, he would take students with him to the woods and hold ceremonies around a fire pit. Remarkably, he asked President MacKenzie for permission to use the chapel for the ordination of a new bishop. Having an ecumenical streak, MacKenzie gave his permission, failing to ask what church was doing the ordination.

How good a practitioner of Devil worship this professor was we have no way of knowing. He was not, however, stellar in his classroom performances. Once President MacKenzie heard about the professor's spiritual practices and then learned about his abysmal teaching, he resolved to relieve him of his classroom duties. For some reason, MacKenzie was loathe to fire anyone. Hence, he appointed this professor as Assistant to the President and gave him an empty office on the third floor of Crawford Hall. The next year he was given an additional assignment as an assistant for development. At the end of that year, the professor was 65, and thus, not given a new contract. He was retired.

This defrocked professor did not take his involuntary retirement lying down. He joined three other faculty members, who were also retired at age 65, in a lawsuit to regain their jobs on the theory that they had defacto tenure. The College's teaching contracts had always stated that the contract was for one year. After a trial and an appeal these professors lost their case. As for the aforementioned professor, it's worth noting, that students "in the know" were afraid to walk by the vine-covered brick house in which the retired professor lived.

It may be that knowledge of the professor's spiritual habits stimulated another unusual spiritual practice on the campus: Exorcism. Each branch of Christianity has its own view of this power to drive the Devil or demons from a person or place. Knowledge of the above professor's habits may have stimulated another professor to find a way to drive the alleged or actual demons from the campus, perhaps even out of the lives of campus residents. The faculty exorcist being referred to here held to the beliefs of the Charismatic tradition. Their practices are somewhat different than those of Roman Catholics, for example. (Interested parties need to look up the exorcist practices of a particular branch of Christianity that interests them.) For our purposes, we note that student reports over several decades stated that the exorcist professor talked frequently in his classes about his exorcist events, even enlisting students to "learn" how to do it. He also told his students that he saw spaceships from another planet.

As for the impact of the two spiritual practices discussed here on the soul of the College, the result is obvious. The professors' practices over a decade or more could only injure the already weakened condition of the soul by the mid-1970s. The Devil worshiper's dismissal surely took the most powerful demonic practices off the campus. No doubt, the female student groups that followed his views soon disintegrated and/or were graduated.

Exorcism on the campus matched a wave of exorcism in the culture late in the 20th century. As for its impact on the campus, and thus, on the soul of the College, it's difficult to say. Was exorcism a positive force in the face of evil on the campus? Most branches of Christianity believe that fervent prayer restrains evil of all types. It may be conjectured that the solid Christian character of the campus in recent times has suppressed the need for additional attempts to exorcise what evil remains.

* * * *

Soon after Charles MacKenzie arrived and took up his duties as President and stated that his mission was two-fold—to bring a Christian perspective to the intellectual life of the College and to rectify student behavior, he was met immediately with substantial opposition. We have made this point before, but here we want to sketch some of the forms this hostile opposition took. The source of this opposition was among the faculty President Harker hired in his rush to correct the school's accreditation problems, a group supported by Dean Kring.

An event that is surely astonishing emerged from this faculty opposition. These opponents persuaded a young and gifted professor to begin calling the President's residence in the middle of the night and say nothing, but breathe heavily. He made similar calls to the Foster residence. This went on intermittently for weeks. Finally, upon hearing about it, the President of the Board, Albert Hopeman, decided to act. He instructed President MacKenzie to contact ATT and set up a wiretap to trap the caller. After some weeks the calls were tracked to the professor in question. A condition of the wiretap was the College's agreement to prosecute the caller if and when caught. Once the caller was known, MacKenzie persuaded ATT to allow the College to fire the offender in place of a prosecution.

As a footnote to this incident, we note that retired President Harker was visited by two senior members of the Board of Trustees and asked to use his influence to tamp down the hostility of the offending faculty. Some familiar with this situation have suggested that the Trustees implied that they might go public with this matter if it did not change. Apparently, it quieted down, though a simmering opposition to President MacKenzie's reforms among some faculty continued for years. Eventually most of the opposition was replaced by new, younger, better educated (virtually all possessed an earned Doctorate), Christian faculty.

* * * *

Early in President MacKenzie's tenure an underground student newspaper appeared on campus called the *Diogenes Forum* (named after the Greek thinker Diogenes, known for his philosophy of cynicism, 404-323 BC). The paper's purpose was to criticize the administration and the newly appointed faculty. After months of operation, an enterprising student got the bright idea to track down the source of the paper. Eventually he had some leads and decided he had the right person in mind. It so happened that while most students were on break, our sleuth found the dorm room door of his suspect open. He entered and searched the room for a considerable time. Before he left there, he saw the student's Bible on the desk and paged through it. To his surprise, there he found all the data on note cards about the operation of the *Forum*, including notes from faculty who opposed the Administration.

Imaginative sleuth that he was, he decided to create a fake edition of the *Diogenes Forum*, complete with the names of the staff and faculty "advisor." The *coup de grace* was a fake editorial which confessed that the publication was a ruse. The editorial was, of course, written by the sleuth. Hundreds of copies of the fake paper were distributed across the campus and one was taped to the College President's office door. A few days later the sleuth and the actual editor both arrived in Dr. Sparks' Constitutional Law classroom. Before class began, Professor Sparks announced to the class that they had a budding newspaper editor in their midst. The fake edition of the paper was the last edition.

* * * *

Drugs had been a staple of party life on the campus for years before MacKenzie arrived. The practiced continued. Some years after becoming Dean of Students, Foster received word from MacKenzie that the

Trustees had agreed to a request by the State Police that an undercover drug officer be allowed to work on campus. The agent played the role of an in-house painter which allowed him to move from building to building from time to time. He looked the part and played the part of a student well. He soon met many students and talked easily with them. A student even invited him home for Thanksgiving.

    The State Police were of the opinion that Grove City College was the center of a drug distribution ring that served several other colleges in the region. Eventually, it was time for a raid. Notice came to Student Affairs that a squad of drug officers would meet at McDonalds at 9:00 one evening, moving from there to specific dorm rooms. They came, arresting about a half dozen students. When the dust settled, Grove City College was not the center of a drug distribution ring in the area; several Grovers did, however, serve some time in jail for personal possession and distribution. Drug activity on campus slowed down—for a while.

* * * *

    Drug use continued to be a problem, especially marijuana. Dean Foster and his assistants were constantly on the lookout for signs of it. During College breaks his staff would tour dorms and check rooms that they suspected housed marijuana plants. They were often surprised at how many plants, or gardens of plants, they found. The pot detectives soon began to carry small spray bottles filled with bleach or some other chemical that would act as an herbicide. A squirt of this "magic" juice would begin the wilting of the plants. Upon returning from vacations, some of these students wondered what happened to their plants. Some thought that they needed to learn how to be better farmers.

On other occasions students would become suspicious that a raid on their rooms was about to occur. In the early days of the Foster regime, the fraternity RAs would tip off the students. With this suspicion, some students would throw their pot plants out the window. When spring came, a fine crop of marijuana plants could be found growing in the soil near the foundation of many dorms. When asked about it, none of the students had any idea about how the plants got there.

* * * *

No doubt many alumni could add additional accounts of people and events that show the same flavor evident in the items presented here. Indeed, that could be the subject of a whole book. In fact, if such alums would like to send along interesting stories, they would be appreciated. But, we now turn to a few concluding words in an epilogue.

An Epilogue

We indicated in the Prologue that this essay would end once its purpose had been achieved and that purpose was to trace the development of the spiritual life, that is, the soul of the College to recent times. And, when would that be? Being an historical study, it needed to end before it turned into an exercise in journalism. It was clear as the focus of the study moved into the 1990s, as President Combee left office, the end point had been reached.

Most colleges that began as a Christian institution in the 19th century remained that way for decades, but by the middle of the 20th century descended into a condition that intellectually and socially resembled secular, party-oriented state universities. That Grove City College was able to return to its moorings, after a season of tasting the fruits of certain secular practices, is astonishing. Surely this is unique in modern American higher education.

By 1990, the College became recognized for its high quality in the classroom, high test scores of entrants, a lively Christian atmosphere among students, excellent teaching by fully qualified faculty, and all at a cost lower than other private schools. National magazines continuously gave it high rankings. And, unlike most other schools, Grove City College stood for freedom, both Christian freedom and its step-children enumerated in the Bill of Rights.

The College entered another stage in the summer of 2014 when the Board of Trustees appointed the Hon. Paul McNulty as the College's ninth President. In addition to tending to the usual affairs of the College, President McNulty has indicated that he intends to strengthen the "faith and learning" dimension of campus life. He personally became a changed man while at Grove City College, he says, because he learned from professors Foster and Hoffecker as a student in the Religion/Philosophy course, what faith and learning really meant. This experience was greatly expanded upon, says McNulty, in Professor Sparks' Constitutional Law course. In fact, McNulty has been a missionary for the principles of the Religion/Philosophy course during his decades of government service in Washington, even while busy as the Acting Attorney General of the United States.

And now a penultimate word about the College. A mother of two Grove City College graduates recently told me that she tells all her friends that there is only one college to which they should send their children and grandchildren: GROVE CITY COLLEGE! Why? It's the only place, she says, where they will not be ruined by the prevailing secular climate found in state universities and most other private colleges. And I endorse that!

For me personally, it has been an exciting and humbling experience to review and write about my 43-year spiritual odyssey since arriving at the College. And, as part of the Center for Vision & Values, it continues. I must note here, however, that it was by God's Providence, I like to say "Special Providence," that I became acquainted with Grove City College. J. Howard Pew made ALL the difference in my life and that of the College.

Despite some early challenges, discussed in Chapter 5, my time at the College has been gratifying. I trust that God will bless others with the same joy that I have had serving in this corner of His Kingdom. And, from my study of Grove City College I want to say without qualification that the College has never enjoyed such high quality in academic rigor, Christian perspective, and a wholesome, Christ-centered social life than it does now. The founders, and more particularly J. Howard Pew, would be most pleased to see how the College has progressed in these ways, since J. Howard called for reforms in his last significant act as Board Chairman.

There is a bronze likeness of him in the garden to the west of the Chapel. I have a miniature replica of it, thanks to President Jewell, which stands on a bookshelf next to my desk. I smile when I look at it because it reminds me of what a great benefactor he was for the College. And, it recalls to me what a great benefactor he was for me, too, when he set me on a path that led to a lifetime of work at the College. For that, Kathryn and I thank him, with deep affection.

Appendix A

Grove City College Presidents

1. **Isaac Conrad Ketler**
(1884-1913)

2. **Alexander T. Ormond**
(1913-1915)

3. **Weir C. Ketler '08**
(1916-1956)

4. **John Stanley Harker '25**
(1956-1971)

5. **Charles Sherrard MacKenzie**
(1971-1991)

6. **Jerry H. Combee**
(1991-1995)

7. **John H. Moore**
(1996-2003)

8. **Richard G. Jewell '67**
(2003-2014)

9. **Paul J. McNulty '80**
(2014-Present)

Grove City College Chairmen of the Board

1. **James Hunter**
   (1877-1879)

2. **W.A. Young**
   (1880-1882)

3. **T.W. Dale**
   (1883-1888)

4. **John N. White**
   (1889-1891)

5. **Rev. W.J. McConkey**
   (1892-1894)

6. **Joseph Newton Pew**
   (1895-1912)

7. **Fred R. Babcock**
   (1912-1927)

8. **William L. Clause**
   (1928-1931)

9. **John Howard Pew**
   (1931-1971)

10. **Albert A. Hopeman**
    (1972-1998)

11. **J. Paul Sticht**
    (1998-2003)

12. **David R. Rathburn**
    (2003-Present)

Appendix B

"Pine Grove Normal Academy." 1877-78

ANNUAL CATALOGUE

OF THE

OFFICERS, TEACHERS AND STUDENTS

OF THE

Pine Grove Normal Academy,

Pine Grove, Mercer County, Pa.,

FOR THE

ACADEMIC YEAR 1877-78,

AND

CALENDAR FOR 1878-79.

MERCER, PA.
THE MERCER DISPATCH JOB PRINTING OFFICE.
1878.

BOARD OF TRUSTEES.

O. P. McCOY, JOSEPH HUMPHREYS,
N. W. VAN EMAN, M. D., JAMES HUNTER,
J. M. MARTIN, M. D.

OFFICERS.

JAMES HUNTER, President.
J. M. MARTIN, M. D., Secretary.
N. W. VAN EMAN, M. D., Treasurer.

CALENDAR--1878-9.

Fall Term---13 weeks, commences Tuesday, August 13, 1878.
Winter Term—13 weeks, commences Tuesday, Dec. 3, 1878.
Spring Term—12 weeks, commences Tuesday, April 1, 1879.

Teachers.

ISAAC C. KETLER,
Principal and Instructor in Theory of Teaching.

JAMES B. McCLELLAND, A. B.,
Instructor in Latin and Greek.

HOMER J. ROSE,
Instructor in History and Philosophy.

SAMUEL R. McCLELLAND,
Instructor in English Grammar and Rhetoric.

HATTIE SHAW,
Instructor in Arithmetic and Algebra.

JOHN A. COURTNEY,
Instructor in Higher Mathematics.

ROBERT D CRAWFORD,
Instructor in Geography and Penmanship.

EMMA McCONNELL,
Instructor in Instrumental Music.

SHERMAN L. BLACK,
Professor of Vocal Music.

PINE GROVE

STUDENTS.

GENTLEMEN.

NAME.	RESIDENCE.	
Allen, S. R.	London,	Mercer county, Pa.
Allen, J. S.	Balm,	"
Allen, W. J.	London,	"
Allen, Amos B.	East Brook,	Lawrence county, Pa.
Alexander, T. E.	Pardoe,	Mercer county, Pa.
Arbuckle, Perry A.	Balm,	"
Armstrong, T. E.	Wolf Creek,	"
Black, J. G.	London,	"
Boston, S. L.	Mercer,	"
Black, J. A.	Wolf Creek,	"
Breckenridge, W. L.	Pardoe,	"
Breckenridge, John	Pardoe,	"
Black, Elmer	Wolf Creek,	"
Black, Ira C.	London,	"
Ball, A. C.	Hendersonville,	"
Bovard, O. D.	New Hope,	Butler county, Pa.
Bell, J. M.	West Middlesex,	Mercer county, Pa.
Biddle, J. W.	New Wilmington,	Lawrence county, Pa.
Courtney, J. A.	Mercer,	Mercer county, Pa.
Coulter, J. C.	Wolf Creek,	"
Carter, A. B.	Indian Run,	"
Cannon, William H.	Martinsburg,	Butler county, Pa.
Crawford, R. D.	Pardoe,	Mercer county, Pa.
Cunningham, Glenn	Wolk Creek,	"
Courtney, George F.	Mercer,	"
Crawford, James D.	Mercer,	"
Davidson, George A.	Slippery Rock,	Butler county, Pa.
Dickey, S. A.	Jacksville	"
Elrick, J. M.	Harrisville,	"
Gillett, J. C.	Raymilton,	Venango county, Pa.
Gilmer, George	Wolf Creek,	Mercer county, Pa.
Green, David	Harrisville,	Butler county, Pa.
Humphrey, David,	Wolf Creek,	Mercer county, Pa.

NORMAL ACADEMY.

Hunt, J. L.	Memphis,	Butler county, Pa.
Hunter, Matthew	Wolf Creek,	Mercer county, Pa.
Irwin, Thomas	Pardoe,	"
Jacobs, C. H.	Millbrook,	"
Junkin, C. M.	Wolf Creek,	"
James, F. P.	Wolf Creek,	"
Kerr, J. L.	Milledgeville,	"
Kerr, C. C.	Harrisville,	Butler county, Pa.
Locke, Lincoln,	Wolf Creek,	Mercer county, Pa.,
Lamb, George H.	Millbrook,	"
Laughlin, M. F.	Millbrook,	"
McClelland, A. C.	Balm,	"
Montgomery, A. A.	Mercer,	"
McEwen, D. B.	Cool Spring,	"
Montgomery, T. N.	Centertown,	"
McDougall, W. V.	Wolf Creek,	"
Moore, J. N.	Jacksville,	Butler county, Pa.
McCracken, S. L.	London,	Mercer county, Pa.
McDowell, Winfield	Wolf Creek,	"
McConnell, Walker	Volant,	Lawrence county, Pa.
McKee, Ellsworth	Pardoe,	Mercer county, Pa.
Miller, R. J.	Pardoe,	"
Moore, E. W.	Summit City,	Venango county, Pa.
Miller, Jas. E.	Eau Claire,	Butler county, Pa.
Minnich, Charles	Plain Grove,	Lawrence county, Pa.
McCune, Samuel		Venango county, Pa.
McDowell, Lyman	Wolf Creek,	Mercer county, Pa.
Miller, Lewis	Pardoe,	"
Morrow, J. B.	Plain Grove,	Lawrence county, Pa.
Morrison, F. S.	Mercer,	Mercer county, Pa.
McKee, Frank	Clintonville,	Venango county, Pa.
Morrow, J. R. H.	Harrisville,	Butler county, Pa.
McElheny, W. G.	Slippery Rock,	"
McConnell, F. G.	Millbrook,	Mercer county, Pa.
McPherrine, Charles	Parker City,	
Newbury, John	Mercer,	Mercer county, Pa.
Orr, J. C.	Mercer,	"
Park, H. C.	Balm,	"
Patterson, Lewis	Wolf Creek,	"
Pearson, A. E.	London,	"
Redmond, R. E.	North Liberty,	"
Robb, J. F.	Wolf Creek,	"
Rose, William	Wolf Creek,	"
Rose, J. G.	Wolf Creek,	"

PINE GROVE

Rose, H. F.	Wolf Creek,	Mercer county, Pa.
Ralston, E. L.	Slippery Rock,	Butler county, Pa.
Simpson, Jas., Jr.	Wolf Creek,	Mercer county, Pa.
Snyder, M. B.	Slippery Rock,	Butler county, Pa.
Snyder, S. B.	Slippery Rock,	"
Shaw, Jas. H.	Neshannock Falls,	Lawrence county, Pa.
Simcox, J. C.	Summit City,	Venango county, Pa.
Scott, John	New Hope,	Butler county, Pa.
Shields, J. M.	Jacksville,	"
Say, Edgar	Martinsburg,	"
Thompson, William	London,	Mercer county, Pa.
Tharp, W. C.	Slippery Rock,	Butler county, Pa.
Uber, F. G.	London,	Mercer county, Pa.
Van Horn, W. L.	Balm,	"
Van Eman, Clarence	Wolf Creek,	"
Wolfe, George L.	Wolf Creek,	"
White, J. B.	Wolf Creek,	"
White, Elmer E.	Millbrook,	"
Weakley, Jas.	Wolf Creek,	"
Welch, Charles	Wolf Creek,	"
Welsh, W. J.	Six Points,	Butler county, Pa.
Williams, F. B.	Harrisville,	"
Walls, Essington	Balm,	Mercer county, Pa.
Young, Seymor	Wolf Creek,	"

LADIES.

Allen, Mary	Balm,	Mercer county, Pa.
Allen, Maggie J.	Balm,	"
Arbuckle, Minnie	Balm,	"
Armstrong, Fannie	Wolf Creek,	"
Allen, Julia	London,	"
Black, Sadie	Wolf Creek,	"
Bolender, Mellie	Wolf Creek,	"
Black, Jennie	Wolf Creek,	"
Breckenridge, Etta	Pardoe,	"
Breckenridge, Anna	Pardoe,	"
Breckenridge, Eva	Clintonville,	Venango county, Pa.
Breckenridge, Anna	Clintonville,	"
Black, Ella	London,	Mercer county, Pa.
Bagnall, Maggie	Mercer,	"
Bell, Villie	London,	"
Black, Laura	Wolf Creek,	"
Brown, Sadie	Harrisville,	Butler county, Pa.
Bell, Franc	West Middlesex,	Mercer county, Pa.

NORMAL ACADEMY.

Black, Eva	Wolf Creek,	Mercer county, Pa.
Beckwith, K. C.	Harrisville,	Butler county, Pa.
Burns, S. C.	Milledgeville,	Mercer county, Pa.
Braham, S. L.	Harrisville,	Butler county, Pa.
Braham, Mary J.	Harrisville,	"
Bell, Lillie	London,	Mercer county, Pa.
Courtney, Jennie	North Liberty,	"
Cummings, Ella	Wolf Creek,	"
Courtney, Sadie	Mercer,	"
Cunningham, Clara	Wolf Creek,	"
Crawford, Hattie	Eau Claire,	Butler county, Pa.
Cannon, Laura B.	Martinsburg,	"
Dunwiddie, Nannie	Harrisville,	"
Daugherty, Ollie	Wolf Creek,	Mercer county, Pa.
Dodds, Mrs. Mary	Pardoe,	"
Emery, Lulu	Wolf Creek,	"
Emery, Eva	Wolf Creek,	"
Floyd, May	Hilliard,	Butler county, Pa.
George, Maggie	North Liberty,	Mercer county, Pa.
Gilfillan, Flora	North Liberty,	"
Gibson, Alice	Six Points,	Butler county, Pa.
Gill, Jose	Harrisville,	"
Heasley, Mary	Balm	Mercer county, Pa.
Hosack, Maggie	Pardoe,	"
Hosack, Annie	Pardoe,	"
Hall, Maggie	North Hope,	Butler county, Pa.
Huggart, Maggie	Pardoe,	Mercer county Pa.,
Hunter, Susan	Wolf Creek,	"
Hilliard, Alice E.	Hilliard,	Butler county, Pa.
Irons, Aggie	Portersville,	"
Junkin, Mary E.	Wolf Creek,	Mercer county, Pa.
Kinder, Edith,	Wolf Creek,	"
Ketler, Emma	Six Points,	Butler county, Pa,
Love, Lizzie M.	Mercer,	Mercer county, Pa.
Love, Nannie A. (deceased)	Mercer,	"
Ligo, Linna	Indian Run,	"
Lane, Dora	Hayt's Corners,	Seneca county, N. Y.
Montgomery, Mary E.	Mercer,	Mercer county, Pa.
Montgomery, Jennie	Mercer,	"
McCole, Eva	Wolf Creek,	"
McDougall, Nannie	Wolf Creek,	"
McDougall, Mary J.	Wolf Creek,	"
Miller, Mattie	Centertown,	"
McGonnagle, Mary	North Liberty,	"

PINE GROVE

McMillen, Clara	Mercer,	"
Maxwell, Flora	Wolf Creek,	"
McMillen, Sadie	Wolf Creek,	"
Miller, Ellen	Harrisville,	Butler county, Pa.
Miller, Maggie J.	Harrisville,	"
Monroe, Effie J.	Wolf Creek,	Mercer county, Pa.
Montgomery, Melissa	Pardoe,	"
Minnich, Alice	Plain Grove,	Lawrence county, Pa.
Morrow, Carrie	Mercer,	Mercer county, Pa.
McDowell, Sarah	Centertown,	"
Minnich, Emma	New Wilmington,	Lawrence county, Pa.
McCune, Linna	Wolf Creek,	Mercer county, Pa.
McNees, Rosa	Jacksville,	Butler county, Pa.
McBride, Lizzie	Witherup,	Venango county, Pa.
McDowell, Lizzie	Wolf Creek,	Mercer county, Pa.
McDowell, S. C.	Millbrook,	"
McWilliams, Dorcas	Mercer,	"
McGonnagle, Tillie	North Liberty,	"
Opre, Ella	Wolf Creek,	"
Pelton, Mary,	Wolf Creek,	"
Pearson, Lila	London,	"
Pifer, Lizzie	London,	"
Redmond, Mime	North Liberty,	"
Rose, Nannie	Wolf Creek,	"
Shaw, Hattie	Neshannock Falls,	Lawrence county, Pa.
Snyder, Mary L.	Slippery Rock,	Butler county, Pa.
Snyder, D. A.	Slippery Rock,	"
Thompson, Maggie,	Centertown,	Mercer county, Pa.
Thompson, Beckie	Centertown,	"
Taylor, Sadie L.	Jacksville,	Butler county, Pa.
Van Eman, Maggie	Wolf Creek,	Mercer county, Pa.
Van Horn, Ida	Balm,	"
Williams, Maggie M.	Harrisville,	Butler county, Pa.
Welch, Jennie	Wolf Creek,	Mercer county, Pa.
Weakley, Franc E.	Wolf Creek,	"
Williams, Fannie	Mercer	"
White, Jose	Millbrook,	"
Walls, Annie	Wolf Creek,	"

NORMAL ACADEMY.

Preparatory Department.

SENIOR CLASS.

NAME.	RESIDENCE.	
Allen, S. R.	London,	Mercer county, Pa.
Allen, J. S.	Balm,	"
Boston, S. L.	Mercer,	"
Breckenridge, W. L.	Pardoe,	"
Courtney, J. A.	Mercer,	"
Laughlin, M. F.	Millbrook,	"
Thompson, William	London,	"
Van Eman, Clarence	Wolf Creek,	"

JUNIOR CLASS.

Black, J. G.	London,	Mercer county, Pa.
Black, J. E.	Wolf Creek,	"
Bovard, O. D.	New Hope,	Butler county, Pa.
Carter, A. B.	Indian Run,	Mercer county, Pa.
Dickey, S. A.	Jacksville	Butler county, Pa.
Elrick, J. M.	Harrisville,	"
Hunt, J. L.	Memphis,	"
Junkin, C. M.	Wolf Creek,	Mercer county, Pa.
Kerr, J. L.	Milledgeville,	"
Moore, J. N.	Jacksville,	Butler county, Pa.
McCracken, S. L.	London,	Mercer county, Pa.
McDowell, Winfield	Wolf Creek,	"
McConnell, Walker	Volant,	Lawrence county, Pa.
Moore, E. W.	Summit,	Venango county, Pa.
Morrow, J. B.	Plain Grove,	Lawrence county, Pa.
McElheny, W. G.	Slippery Rock,	Butler county, Pa.
Morrow, J. R. H.	Harrisville,	"
Rose, J. G.	Wolf Creek,	Mercer county, Pa.
Ralston, E. L.	Slippery Rock,	Butler county, Pa.
Snyder, M. B.	Slippery Rock,	"
Snyder, S. B.	Slippery Rock,	"
Shields, J. M.	Jacksville,	"
Tharp, W. C.	Slippery Rock,	"
Uber, F. G.	London,	Mercer county, Pa.
Van Horn, W. L.	Balm,	"
White, J. B.	Wolf Creek,	"

10 PINE GROVE

Williams, F. B.	Harrisville,	Butler county, Pa.
Black, Ella	London,	Mercer county, Pa.
Black, Sadie	Wolf Creek,	"
Irons, Aggie	Portersville,	Butler county, Pa.
Kinder, Edith,	Wolf Creek,	Mercer county, Pa.
Maxwell, Flora	Wolf Creek,	"
Miller, Ellen	Harrisville,	Butler county, Pa.
Shaw, Hattie	Neshannock Falls,	Lawrence county, Pa.
Taylor, Sadie L.	Jacksville,	Butler county, Pa.
White, Josie	Millbrook,	Mercer county, Pa.

Instrumental Music.

NAME.		RESIDENCE.
Armstrong, Fannie	Wolf Creek,	Mercer county, Pa.
Black, Jennie	Wolf Creek,	"
Hall, Maggie	North Hope,	Butler county, Pa.
Ketler, Emma	Six Points,	"
McNees, Rosa	Jacksville,	"
Monroe, Effie J.	Wolf Creek,	Mercer county, Pa.
Patton, Mamie	Wolf Creek,	"
Taylor, Sadie L.	Jacksville,	Butler county, Pa.

Summary.

Preparatory Department—Senior Class, - - - - 8
                                     Junior Class, - - - - 36
Department of Instrumental Music, - - - - - 8
Normal Department, - - - - - - - 151

    Different students, - - - - - - 203
    Total attendance for the year, 283.

NORMAL ACADEMY.

College Preparatory Course of Study.

FIRST YEAR.

FIRST TERM.—English Grammar. Practical Arithmetic—*Stoddards*. Latin Lessons—*Bullion & Morris'*. Political Geography—*Guyot's*.

SECOND TERM.—English Analysis. Latin Lessons first half of term, Cæsar and Latin Grammar last half of term. U. S. History. Practical Arithmetic—*Stoddard's*.

THIRD TERM.—Cæsar and Latin Grammar. Algebra—*Robinson's*. Greek Lessons and Greek Grammar—*Crosby's*. Physical Geography—*Warren's*.

Exercises daily during the year in Reading and Spelling.

SECOND YEAR.

FIRST TERM.—Cicero—*Chase and Stuart's*. Greek Lessons first half of term, Xenophon's Anabasis and Greek Grammar last half of term. Algebra—*Robinson's*. Etymology, and Historical, Mythological and Geographical Allusions.

SECOND TERM.—Cicero first half of term, Virgil last half of term. Xenophon's Anabasis—*Crosby's*. Algebra—*Ray's Part Second*. Geometry (begun)—*Robinson's*.

THIRD TERM.—Virgil—*Chase & Stuart's*. Homer's Iliad—*Boise's*. Rhetoric and Composition—*Quackenbos'*. Geometry (finished)—*Robinson's*.

During the year daily exercises in reading and spelling.

REMARKS ON PREPARATORY COURSE.

During the past twenty years' history of the school special attention has been paid to the preparation of sudents for college. Almost yearly quite a number of students have left this school, and on examination have universally taken high standing in the Freshman year at college. The almost unexceptionable high character of the students who leave this school for college, both in scholarship and habits, has obtained for the school the *formal recognition* of some of the best colleges near. No other academy in the State has up to the present time been recognized by colleges. This gives to the school here an advantage which no other academy in the State enjoys. A certificate from the faculty here entitles the student to a standing in the Freshman class at the colleges—with which arrangements have been made,—*without further examination.*

The preparatory course is such as is fully up to the requirements of the best colleges, and much beyond the demands of many. The large number of students who prepare here for college makes it possible to give more attention to the collegiate-preparatory work than at many of the best colleges. No student can receive a certificate from the school without first standing a thorough examination on at least all studies of the preparatory course of the college he wishes to enter. The faculty will in no case recommend to any college, whether of those which have recognized this school or of those which have not, any student who cannot sustain, in scholarship and good habits, the character of the school.

Thoroughness in the English branches is one of the leading aims in the preparatory work, and as much attention is paid to that feature of the course as in the regular teachers' course. Each term beginning classes in Latin and Greek are organized. Almost every grade of Latin and Greek classes is found here every term.

TERMS OF ADMISSION.

Those admitted to the preparatory course must pass a satisfactory examination in the work laid down in the first and second terms of the first year of the "Teachers' Course," and must be of an age sufficient to justify them in beginning the regular work of the preparatory course. Students are received at any time into the course who secure their standing by examination on all the branches up to the time they wish to enter. Real equivalents are taken on examination.

NORMAL ACADEMY.

Teachers' Course of Study.

FIRST YEAR.

FIRST TERM.—Practical Arithmetic (from Common Fractions to Percentage.) Grammar, Language Lessons and Composition. Reading and Penmanship. Rudiments of Vocal Music.

SECOND TERM.—Practical Arithmetic (from Percentage to Compound Proportion.) English Grammar and Composition. Political Geography—*Guyot's*. Vocal Music and Penmanship.

THIRD TERM.—Practical Arithmetic (completed)—*Stoddard's*. English Analysis. Political Geography. Vocal Music and Reading. Physiology—*Cutter's*.

Daily drills in spelling throughout the year.

SECOND YEAR.

FIRST TERM.—United States History. Intellectual Arithmetic—*Dean's*. Algebra (begun)—*Robinson's*. Physical Geography—*Warren's* Vocal Music and Penmanship.

SECOND TERM.—United States History. Algebra (completed)—*Robinson's*. School Economy—*Wickersham*. Rhetoric—*Quackenbos'*. Drills in Vocal Music and Reading.

THIRD TERM.—Natural Philosophy—*Wells'*. Geometry—*Robinson's*. Methods of Instruction—*Wickersham* and others. Botany—*Gray*. Vocal Music.

Daily drills throughout the year in spelling.

REMARKS ON TEACHERS' COURSE.

The course of study laid down for teachers has been adopted after much careful consideration of the wants of teachers, and the demands of the common schools and popular education. Nearly twice the time is spent on the common branches here that is required at many other institutions, and with marked success. No subject is passed over until it is fully mastered. Habits of industry, punctuality and dispatch are formed here by teachers which insure them success in teaching. Weekly reviews and examinations in the branches studied are found to be indispensable to those who would obtain a thorough knowledge of what they wish to teach, and it is the only sure method of estimating the progress of each student. Classes are formed each term in Theory of Teaching and Methods of Instruction, and the attention of teachers is constantly directed to the methods of presenting to others the subjects which they study. In the reading room teachers' magazines and journals are to be found for the express purpose of awakening teachers to a sense of the worth and importance of their profession.

NORMAL ACADEMY.

Text Books in Use.

MATHEMATICS.

Arithmetic, Practical—*Stoddard's;* Intellectual—*Dean's.* Algebras—*Robinson's Elementary* and *Ray's Second Part.* Geometry—*Robinson's.* Trigonometry—*Loomis'.* Book-Keeping—*Bryant & Stratton's.*

PHYSICAL SCIENCE.

Natural Philosophy—*Wells'.* Botany—*Gray's School and Field Book.* Physical Geography—*Warren's.* Physiology—*Cutter's.*

LANGUAGES.

English Grammar—All authors. English Readers—*Osgood's,* old series. Latin Grammar—*Harkness'.* Latin Lessons—*Bullion & Morris'.* Cæsar—*Harkness'.* Cicero—*Chase & Stuart's.* Virgil—*Chase & Stuart's.* Greek Grammar—*Crosby's.* Greek Lessons—*Crosby's.* Anabasis—*Crosby's.* Homer's Iliad—*Boise.*

MISCELLANEOUS.

History U. S.—All authors. Political Geography—*Guyot's Grammar School.* School Economy—*Wickersham.* Methods of Instruction—*Wickersham.* Etymology—*Sargent & May's.* Instrumental Music—*Root's Model Organ Method.* Vocal Music—*Encore.*

All text books in use can be had here at publishers' regular retail prices.

Students are requested to bring with them all their text books; if not in use here they are of great value for reference.

Department of Music.

INSTRUMENTAL MUSIC.

In this department, which is under the management of an experienced teacher, students are instructed with great care and patience. Lessons on both organ and piano forte are given. Special attention is paid to beginners to give them a thorough knowledge of the rudiments of music. The rapid progress that is made in instrumental music has made this feature of the school very popular. The course of study varies as to the degree of advancement of those taking lessons. The course embraces twenty-four lessons—two each week. All those taking lessons are required to practice at least one and a half hours each day. For the use of instrument in practicing a small rent is charged.

VOCAL MUSIC AND VOICE CULTURE.

The growing necessity of teaching vocal music in the common schools has led to the addition of this much neglected branch to the course of study which teachers will be required to pursue. During the past year an unusual degree of attention has been given to the instruction of teachers in this very essential branch of education, and with excellent results. Live teachers in the common schools lament their lack of skill in training their pupils in the culture of the voice, and their inability to teach successfully the rudiments of music. The school has been divided into two classes with reference to this end. The first division, consisting of those who have had little or no training in music, and the second consisting of those who are able to read music with ease. In both divisions voice culture is the burden of all effort. In the former division the course of instruction consists of voice culture, oral and written exercises on the scale, and reading. In the latter, voice culture, exercises on the scale, art of singing, psalmody, music reading, and the best method of presenting the subject of vocal drill to pupils in the common schools.

Primary Department.

Each fall term the school will be open to primary students. In this department boys and girls from eight to twelve years of age will be received. They will be under the immediate care of the Principal and one assistant. The large number of students in the Normal and Preparatory departments makes it impossible to do justice to primary students without organizing new classes. This has necessitated the organization of the Primary department. The instruction of boys and girls in the rudiments of the common branches will be careful and exact. Special attention will be paid to the health and habits of all. Spelling, reading, penmanship, grammar, geography and arithmetic, together with daily drills in the rudiments of vocal music, will be the principal branches of this department.

The object of this new feature is to give to primary students of the public schools the advantage of thorough instruction in the elements of the common branches, to stimulate the young to correct habits of study, to give to them the advantages of drills in music and penmanship, which they do not enjoy in the public schools, and to enable the school to be graded to the best interests of all.

The text books used will be the same as those used in the public schools of this place. Those coming from a distance should bring all their text books with them, and if not in use here they can be used for reference.

The tuition in this department is $3 per term, or $1.25 per month.

Students of this department will be subject to the same regulations as those of other departments. All will be expected to attend devotional exercises in the morning, and every precaution will be taken that the influences with which they are surrounded will be such as will insure their intellectual and moral growth.

General Remarks.

LOCATION AND HISTORY.

Pine Grove Normal Academy, located at Pine Grove, Pa., on the Shenango and Allegheny railroad, has long enjoyed the reputation of being one of the best schools of the kind in Western Pennsylvania Organized in 1858, it is now entering on its twenty-first year. Feeling the need of a school at which young men and women of this vicinity and adjoining neighborhoods might receive a thorough business education, and at the same time a school which would extend to young men preparing for the professions the advantages of Collegiate Preparatory Instruction, an effort was made to accomplish these ends. Accordingly Prof. Richard M. Thompson, now Rev. Thompson, of Illinois, was called on to take charge of the school, and by his efficient management the experiment proved a success. Soon after Rev. Thompson left to engage in his preferred field of labor, and was followed by several other gentlemen, who contributed largely to the success of the school, among whom were Prof. S. F. Thompson (now attorney at law in Mercer, Pa.), Rev. William T. Dickson (late deceased), and Rev. Ethan McMichael. In 1864, Rev. Dickson and his wife, Mrs. Dickson, took charge of the school, and for eleven years labored earnestly and in every direction, very successfully, to promote the usefulness of the school. During this time the patronage of the school greatly increased, and its influence began to be felt throughout Western Pennsylvania. Hundreds of young men and women throughout the western part of the State have attended school here, and have received, in whole or in part, a good business education. Many are filling positions of trust in almost every department of life. Some have distinguished themselves at the bar, and many are preaching very acceptably the Gospel of Christ. At college those who have prepared here have shown themselves in no respect inferior to students from other institutions, but in many cases leaders both in class and on the rostrum.

The condition of the school was never better than at present. Within the past three years the facilities of the school have been largely increased. A large brick school hall has been erected. The trustees of the Presbyterian church have donated the use of the church for chapel exercises. A reading room has been furnised with the best literary, religious and scientific magazines and journals of the

NORMAL ACADEMY.

day. During the present school year the reference library has received valuable additions. A large boarding hall, for the accommodation of students who wish to board themselves or board on the clubbing system, has been erected, which is under the direct supervision of the teachers of the school.

The school has received the *formal recognition* of some of the best colleges near, which enables students who prepare for college here to enter Freshman class *without further examination*. Two courses of study have been adopted, the Collegiate-Preparatory course and the Teachers' course. Both extend through two years. Both senior and junior classes of the preparatory department are large, and many teachers are fitting themselves for the exercise of greater skill in the school room, both by the study of the branches themselves and by the study of the best methods of presenting them to students.

The department of Music, which is under the care of able instructors, has become one of the leading features of the school.

The attendance has been gradually increasing. The total attendance for this year up to the present time is over two hundred and eighty, being a normal increase over the preceding year.

Many new improvements for the advantage of the school are contemplated. The plan for another boarding hall has been under the contemplation of some of the citizens of the place, and the erection of other buildings for the accommodation of class recitations is now under the consideration of the leading citizens.

The teaching force of the school has been largely increased for the year 1878-9, as will be seen from the addition of new names to the list of teachers.

DESIGN OF THE INSTITUTION.

It is the design of this school to fit young men and women for college, and to prepare those who desire to teach to do good work in the school room; to enable those preparing for college to accomplish the greatest amount of work in the shortest possible time; to give to all a thorough and practical business education; to secure to every young man and woman the advantage of literary and forensic drill; to secure to hundreds of young men and women throughout Western Pennsylvania the benefit of thorough instruction in the branches taught in the common and collegiate preparatory schools; to create in the minds of the youth a thirst for knowledge; to stimulate in students healthy and vigorous activity in the right direction; to aid all in forming correct habits of living and thinking, and to incite in their minds a love for the true, beautiful and the good as developed in nature and art, and in the acts of men.

LATIN AND GREEK.

The instruction in Latin and Greek is careful and thorough; the attention of the student is constantly directed to the construction of the sentence. In the noun, the rules for its construction, and in the verb, the rules for sequence of tenses and the correct translation of the subjunctive and optative modes, are incessantly applied. Weekly reviews give to the students a familiarity with the Latin and Greek text, that they experience no difficulty in reading, at the close of the term, all the Greek and Latin passed over at sight. Latin and Greek composition is one part of the work. A knowledge of quantity in Latin, to enable the student to scan all the poetry he reads, and a knowledge of accent in Greek sufficient for the student to properly accent all the words used in exercises in composition, are required. The amount of Latin and Greek read varies. More attention is paid to the quality than to the quantity of the reading. In Latin, from four to six books of Roman history, with some fables, etc., from three to four books of Cæsar's Commentaries, from three to four orations of Cicero, from three to five books Virgil's Æneid; and in Greek, one and one-half terms in Greek Reader, from two to three books Xenophon's Anabasis, and two books Homer's Iliad, is the requirement.

BOOK-KEEPING AND PENMANSHIP.

Book-keeping in all the details of Single and Double Entry, both as a science and an art, receives special attention.

Penmanship. which is so much neglected in many schools, receives careful and skillful attention by an experienced teacher.

LECTURES TO STUDENTS.

During the year several addresses have been delivered to the students by prominent educators of this section, among whom were Rev. David McAllister, of Philadelphia, subject, "The Bible, its relation to education and National prosperity;" Rev. Lucius H. Bugbee, D. D., President of Allegheny College, subject, "Travel, with sketches and observations," and Rev. E. T. Jeffers, D. D., President of Westminster College, subject,-——

During the coming year the advantages which students enjoy in this respect will be increased.

LITERARY SOCIETIES.

Two well-sustained literary societies are connected with the school, the "Conabor" and the "Bryant." All the students are required to take advantage of the benefits arising from these societies. The number of students who have taken part, voluntarily, in these societies, has exceeded fifty in each, during the past year. All attest to the great benefits derived from these two most important auxiliaries of the school. No student is exempt from performing the part assigned him in the society, once in two weeks. Every effort is made to secure to all the advantages of literary and forensic drill.

READING ROOM.

A Reading Room has been furnished with some of the leading scientific, literary and religious papers, and educational and literary magazines and reviews. Students have daily access to this reading matter free of charge. The Reading Room has become an indispensable auxiliary in the school. Every term new attractions are added to it, and students are beginning to realize how impossible it is to improve their time successfully without the very important helps provided by a well furnished Reading Room.

REFERENCE LIBRARY.

Within the past year the aids of students have been largely improved by valuable additions to the library in the form of books of reference, among which are American Cyclopedia, Chambers' Encyclopedia, pronouncing, geographical and classical dictionaries, besides bound volumes of magazines, religious, scientific and educational journals. This library is in constant use. The instruction in class and in chapel is such as to lead students daily to seek the library for reference. This library is being enlarged as fast as the finances of the school will permit.

COLLEGE RECOGNITION.

The Normal Academy has received formal recognition from Westminster and Allegheny colleges, and arrangements will soon be effected with other institutions near, by which students who prepare here can enter the Freshman class at college without further examination.

RELIGIOUS EXERCISES.

School is begun each day with devotional exercises. The chapel meetings are the most highly prized exercises of the school. Both teachers and students look forward to the morning meetings with pleasure. So strongly have the students become attached to these meetings that no effort is needed to secure prompt attendance. After the devotional exercises each morning a half hour is spent in discussion of various topics by the students, lessons on the biography of noted men and women, together with analyses of their characters and the elements which entered into the makeup of their success in life. Historical essays on foreign lands of ancient and modern times, essays on historical and mythological allusions, and a careful study of the current events of the times, constitute a part of the very interesting and profitable exercises at chapel.

PRAYER MEETINGS AND PREACHING.

Prayer meeting is held three times each week at the Presbyterian church and twice each week at the M. E. church, at which the students are always welcome. A number of churches of different denominations are within easy access of the school. Students are expected to attend preaching at least once on Sabbath. The influences with which students are surrounded are good. The morality of the town is proverbial. No licensed houses or saloons are in this vicinity. The location of the place is healthy and heartsome.

NORMAL DEBATING CLUB.

Once each week the debating society, which is largely attended by the young men of the school, meets for the discussion of some subject which has previously been selected. All are required to participate in these discussions. Impromptu speeches on subjects assigned by the President, volunteer orations and declamations, and friendly criticisms on matter and manner of addresses constitute the order of exercises. The best students of the school take great interest in this means of improving themselves in thinking and in speaking.

NORMAL ACADEMY.

Tuition.

Primary,	per term,	$3 00
Intermediate,	"	6 50
Higher English and Classics,	"	8 00
Instrumental Music,	"	10 00

No contingent fee is charged. No extra charge is made for vocal music. No charge for use of reading matter and library.

No reduction from above rates on account of absence a part of term unless by previous arrangement, except in case of sickness, and then no reduction will be made for less than two weeks' absence.

Boarding.

Boarding in private families, everything found, $2.50 to $3.00 per week; from Monday until Friday, $2.00 per week. Students, by clubbing, can reduce these rates. By this plan students furnish their own room, find eatables, and pay from 60 to 75 cents for the cooking per week. Many students board themselves, and by so doing enjoy the conveniences of home at a much less cost than by either of the other methods. Rooms for those who wish to board on the clubbing plan, or to board themselves, can be rented at very reasonable rates. Unfurnished rooms rent at $1 per month per student. In the boarding hall, which is under the care of the teachers of the school, unfurnished rooms can be had at $1 per month per student. Those furnished with table, cupboard, chairs and bedstead, 50 cents extra a term per student. A limited number of stoves can be had by those who come from a distance at a small additional charge. Students board only at those places approved of by the Principal.

Those who purpose going to school should address the Principal in good time for rooms, boarding, &c. Those coming here for the first time should invariably write to the Principal for boarding or rooms before starting, that there may be no trouble in finding places suitable.

ISAAC C. KETLER, *Principal*,
PINE GROVE, MERCER COUNTY, PA.

Appendix C
"Campus and Dormitory Customs and Standards." 1921

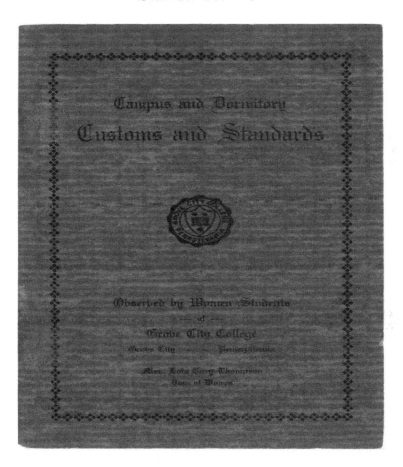

Text from Cover (above):

Campus and Dormitory
Customs and Standards

Observed by Women Students
Grove City College
Grove City, Pennsylvania
Mrs. Lori Cory-Thompson
Dean of Women

INDEX

	Page	Section	Paragraph
Appointment House Council	4	V	8
After Lights	4	V	13
All Lights Out	5	V	14
Autoing	6	V	31
Assessment	6	V	33
Attitude Toward Waiters	13	IX	1
Answering Whistles	15	XIV	1
Buying Guest Tickets	10	VIII	4
Baths After Lights	4	V	12
Bookcase Magazines	5	V	25
Concise Statement	3	I	2
Comradeship	3	II	1
Calling From Floor to Floor	5	V	18
Current Magazine Issues	5	V	23
Closing of Doors	5	V	28
Care of Bath Rooms	7	V	49
Cottage Girls	10	VII	1-5
Cards for Cottage Girls	10	VII	1
Charge for Trays	12	X	3
Critical Attitude	13	XI	3
Conversation at Table	13	XI	5
Conversational Responsibility	13	XI	6
Changing Tables	13	XI	7
Condition of Room	14	VIII	1
Callers to Leave Promptly	10	VI	28
Dignified Manner	3	III	
Downtown Limit	7	V	50
Dancing	9	VII	26
Daytime Tablet Signing	8	VI	6
Dismissing Escorts Promptly	8	VI	13
Dinner Engagements	9	VI	20
Disturbance After Lights	7	V	51
Evening Guests	8	VI	30
Elimination of Recreation Period	9	VI	21
Extra Light Period	14	VII	1
Fire Escape Misuse	6	V	30
Farewell Vespers	6	V	37
Foregathering	7	VI	2
First Showing of Movie	14	VII	5
Forgetting Things	14	VIII	2
Frequency of Guests	10	VIII	1
Grouping	14	XI	19
Going Down Town After Engagements	9	VI	15
Good Standing	10	VIII	2
Guest Tickets	10	X	5
Gives Orders, Heads	13	XI	13
Gives Signals, Heads	13	XI	14
General Statements	3	I	1
Good Taste	3	III	2
Honors	6	V	38
Holidays	11	IX	2
Hours of Meals	12	X	1
Heads and Opposites	13	XI	8
Ignorance of Regulations	3	I	3
Infraction of Regulations	4	V	4
Introductory Guests	14	XI	17
Loafing and Loitering	3	III	4

	Page	Section	Paragraph
List Posted	6	V	38
Laundry Allowance	6	XI	41
Laundry Limit	6	V	42
Library Hours	8	VI	9
Length of Stay	11	VIII	7
Loyalty to Regulations	11	VIII	9
Leaving a Party Early	9	VI	24
Leaves Dining Room First (Head)	13	XI	15
Leaving Town at Once	14	VIII	4
Laws of Hospitality	15	XIV	2
Manner of Walking with Man	3	III	3
Membership (House Council)	4	V	1
Meetings (House Council)	4	V	2
Magazine Regulations	5	V	22
Manner of Entering Dining Room	14	XI	20
Maids Hours	5	V	26
Marking Laundry	6	V	43
Mid-Week Social Activities	9	VI	16
Movie Privilege	9	VI	17
Maintain Standards (Head)	13	XI	12
Morning Greetings	14	XI	18
Movie Privilege (Exam Period)	14	XII	4
Marking Baggage	14	XIII	3
Necessity of Rules and Regulations	3	I	1
New Regulations	4	V	6
Number of Engagements	8	VI	14
Organizations	8	VI	8
Overnight Privileges	11	IX	10
Obligatory Breakfast	12	X	8
Promptness at Parties	9	VI	25
Phone Calls, Postage Due	5	V	15
Past Issues Magazines	5	V	24
Placing Linen in Corridor	6	V	44
Permission Cards	10	VII	3
Promptness—Cottage Girls	10	VII	4
Quietness	4	V	10
Room Inspection	6	V	35
Reporting to Mrs. Blair	6	V	40
Replacing Furniture	6	VI	53
Returning from Library	8	VI	11
Reporting After Parties	9	VI	23
Reserving Chairs	14	XI	21
Recreation Period	8	VI	7
Remaining in Library	8	VI	10
Remaining Away From Meals	12	X	4
Reports Absentees (Head)	13	XI	11
Recreation Period Eliminated	14	XII	3
Receiving Callers	5	XIII	5
Serious Cases	4	V	5
Shoes	4	V	11
Shades Lowered	5	V	17
Smoking	7	V	48
Shopping Excursions	7	V	52
Stairway Seats	7	V	54
Silver G Pins	6	V	36
Study Hours	7	VI	1
Seniors Signing Up	8	VI	5
Special Movies	9	VI	18

(Index Continued on Page 16)

I. GENERAL STATEMENTS

1 Necessity of Rules and Regulations — In order to maintain the standards upon which our College prides itself, it is necessary to have well defined rules and regulations, as well as to have a clear understanding of our traditions, which years of consistent effort have bequeathed to us.

2 Concise Statement — The customs, rules and regulations will be stated concisely and without special elaboration.

This simplicity of statement will be relied upon to impress them clearly upon everyone's mind.

3 Ignorance of Regulations No Excuse — Ignorance of regulations will not be accepted as an excuse for their infringement.

II. SOCIAL AND SCHOLASTIC RELATIONS

1 Comradeship — A general social and scholastic comradeship between men and women students is both natural and desirable.

2 Scholastic Hours — Scholastic hours should be free of all social demands.

3 Social Opportunities — Ample opportunities for the mingling of men and women students socially are provided.

III. CAMPUS STANDARDS

1 Dignified Manner — A dignified and quiet manner is required.

2 Good Taste — All students are expected to possess and exhibit good taste and good breeding in all their relations as regards the general life of the Campus.

3 Manner of Walking — Clinging to the arm of a man, or having him cling to that of a girl, is in wretched taste and very silly.

4 Loafing and Loitering — Loafing and loitering, either on or off the Campus, is not countenanced.

IV. DORMITORY MATTERS

1 Time For Securing Permission, Etc. — The Dean will be in her office immediately before and after meals (except before breakfast) to attend to guest tickets, tray orders, permissions of all sorts, apologies for lateness or absence from meals, and any matters needing her attention.

She is available at any time for discussion of any matters which anyone may wish to take up with her, excepting between the hours of 1 and 3 P. M.

V. COLONIAL HOUSE COUNCIL

1 Membership — The Colonial House Council is composed of:
House Council President—Senior.
Advisory Committee—Two Seniors.
Cabinet—All Seniors.
Five Juniors.
Three Sophomores.
One Colonial Freshman.
One Representative from each Cottage.

2 Meetings — The Council meets regularly once a week, at a time decided upon by themselves.

3 Deliberations — At these meetings all matters having to do with the interests, either in or out of he dormitory, of the Colonial girls, are taken up, discussed and acted upon.

4 Infraction of Regulations — Infractions of rules and regulations are to be reported to the House Council President or to some member of the Council with the request that the Council take the matter under advisement and decide upon he action to be adopted.

5 Serious Cases — In serious cases consultation with the Dean is customary before a final decision is arrived at.

6 New Regulations — New regulations will be adopted by the House Council as necessity presents itself and after conferring with the Dean.

7 Rotation — The House Council, as concerns its underclass members, rotates during the year thus offering training in responsibility to a greater number.

8 Appointment — The members of the House Council are appointed by the Dean.

9 Vespers — Vespers occur on Tuesday and Thursday evenings immediately after dinner. Attendance is obligatory and no plans must be made to interfere.

10 Quietness — Quietness must be maintained as far as possible in the dormitories.

11 Shoes — Shoes are not to be worn after lights flash nor before the Rising Gong.

12 Baths — Baths are not to be taken after lights nor before the Rising Gong.

13 After Lights — There is to be no talking above a whisper after 10:45 P. M., nor before the Rising Gong.

14 All Lights Out	There must be no lights after 10:45 P. M.
15 Phone Calls and Postage Due	Phone calls, postage due, etc., will be posted on slip in side coridor. Postage due may be left on mail table for postman.
16 Lights Flashed	Lights will be flashed on week days at 10:30 P. M., and out at 10:45 P. M. Sundays, 15 minutes earlier.
17 Shades Lowered	All shades are to be lowered when the electric lights come on.
18 Calling From One Floor to Another	There must be no calling from one floor to another or one part of the building to another.
19 Talking Out of Windows	There must be no calling out of windows to anyone below.
20 Use of Musical Instruments	The piano and other instruments may be used as follows: Immediately after breakfast until recitation bell. From 12:10 until 1 P. M. From 5 until 7:15 P. M. Sundays, not before 12:30 P. M. and from then until 2:00 P. M. 5 to 7:30 P. M.
22 Magazine Regulations	The Magazine Tablet will be found on the table by the magazine rack.
23 Current Issues	Current Issues are in green cloth covers. They are never to be taken from the social rooms.
24 Past Issues	Past Issues are those in the press board covers. They may be taken from social room for 24 hours. Names of girl and date of taking, must be recorded in Magazine Tablet and cancelled upon their return.
25 Bookcase Magazines	Magazines in the book cases may be taken to the rooms and kept as long as desired. Please record same.
26 Maids' Hours	The hall maid attends to calling girls to the phone, carrying messages, etc., until 8:00 P. M.
27 Not Sleeping Out of One's Own Room	One must never sleep out of her own room without special permission. This permission may be secured at any time. No permission to sleep out of one's dormitory will be granted.
28 Closing of Doors	All doors, except the one opposite Ivy Chapel, are closed at 6:00 P. M.
29 Use of Laundry	The Colonial students' laundry is available until 6:00 P. M.

30	Mis-use of Fire Escapes	In case the fire escapes are used for any purpose other than the one for which they are intended, the offender will be promptly and drastically dealt with.
31	Autoing	Autoing is strictly by permission.
32	Evening Autoing	Autoing in the evening is considered undesirable.
33	Assessment	An assessment of $3.00 a year is paid by each girl.
34	Use of This Money	This money is used to take care of all expenses incurred by the girls for special needs; flowers in case of illness or bereavement, special gifts, magazine subscription, social affairs, endowment subscription, etc.
35	Room Inspection	Every room will be inspected once a week. A strict record will be kept.
36	Silver G Pin	Seniors who have made a satisfactory record throughout the course will be awarded the silver G pin at Farewell Vespers.
37	Farewell Vespers	Farewell Vespers will occur on the last Friday before Commencement.
38	Honors	Upon this occasion the Honor List will be read. This will include the names of all those who have throughout the year made some special contribution to the interests of the Colonial life.
39	List Posted	The Honor List will be posted.
40	Reporting to Mrs. Blair	Anything concerning the needs of the room, plumbing, furniture, lights, linen, etc., is to be reported to the Matron, Mrs. Blair.
41	Laundry Allowance	The Colonial laundry will take care of the following linen without extra charge: one sheet, single; one pillow slip, face towels, bath towels.
42	Limit	No wash cloths, runners, or anything else will be taken.
43	Marking	All linen is to be plainly marked with the name of owner in indelible ink.
44	Placing in Corridor	Linen is to be laid in neat piles by doors in corridors on Sunday evening. It must not be put there during the day on account of possible guests.
45	Tacking and Pasting on Walls	a No tacking or pasting on walls in any part of the dormitory is allowed. b It will not be permitted to use tacks or nails which may happen to be left in the walls.

c Everything must be suspended from the moulding.

d Anyone failing to observe this regulation will be fined $1.00 for every tack hole and for each paste mark.

This is a rule of the General Administration.

46 Negligees	Negligee costumes are not to be worn in the Social Rooms before 9:30 p. m.
47 Unlocking Fire Escapes	Fire escape exits must not be unlocked after locked by maid at 6 P. M.
48 Smoking	Smoking by women students, either inside or outside of the dormitories is forbidden. Offenders will be drastically dealt with.
49 Care of Bathrooms	The main has been instructed not to clean bathrooms which are unreasonably untidy.
50 Downtown Time Limit	Going downtown is under the 20 minute regulation, except for legitimate shopping. There must be no loafing at any time.
51 Disturbance After Lights	In case it is necessary to return a second time to quiet noise after lights in any part of the dormitory the offenders place themselves under the penalty decided upon by the House Council—remaining in the dormitory for three consecutive nights. Cottage girls are under the same restriction.
52 Shopping Excursions	Shopping excursions out of town in mid-week must start after luncheon and return in time for dinner. A personal report must be made upon return.
53 Replacing Furniture	Furniture in the social rooms is to be replaced in regular order after guests have left on receiving evenings.
54 Stairway Seats	No one is to sit farther up on the stairway than the fourth step.

VI. CONCERNING EVENING PRIVILEGES

1 Study Hour	Evening study hour begins at 7:15 every evening except Saturday and Sunday.
2 No Foregathering	The interest of all requires that there be no gathering in groups either in social or private rooms during study hour.
	All conditions must be conducive to study.

3 Evening Guests	Out-of-dorm girls are not permitted to go to girls' rooms during evening study hour except by permission.
4 Corridor Tablets	Everyone, except Seniors, leaving the dormitories in the evening is to sign up on the corridor tablet, cancelling when returning.
5 Seniors	Seniors are to sign up if wishing to be out later than 9 o'clock.
6 Daytime Signing	Everyone except Seniors is to sign up during the daytime if wishing to leave the Campus.
7 Recreation Period	A recreation period occurs from 10 to 10:30 P. M. Immediately upon its conclusion the dormitories must become quiet.
8 Organizations	All those who are members of College organizations which meet in the evening may attend without special permission. Any wishing to visit them must have special permission.
9 Library	Evening Library Hours are as follows: Freshmen—7 to 8 P. M. Sophomores and Juniors—7 to 8:30 P. M. Seniors—7 to 9 P. M.
10 Remaining in Library	In case one should fail to remain in the Library when she is supposed to be there, her case will be reported to the House Council.
11 Returning from Library	None may stay later at the library than the limit specified, without permission. In emergency cases, word may be sent to me to explain tardiness.
12 Town Privilege	Anyone may go down within the hours specified above. No one must remain down town longer than 20 minutes. Permission must be obtained.
13 Dismissing Escorts Promptly	Upon returning to the dormitory, courtesy demands that the escort bring the young woman to the door and leave promptly. Standing in conversation at varying distances from this entrance is a silly and undesirable custom.
14 Number of Engagements	Seniors are allowed three evening engagements a week with men. One may be a mid-week movie. Underclass girls are allowed two evening engagements with men which are to come at the week-end. Men may come in after Sunday evening church.

15	Going Down Town After Engagements	Underclass girls are not allowed to go down town after entertainments, except on Saturday evening.
16	Mid-Week Social Activities	No mid-week social activities are allowed.
17	Movie Privilege	Underclass girls are allowed movie privilege once a week, on Saturday evening except on very special occasions.
18	Special Movies	In order to see a notable movie a special permission is now and then granted. When this is the case, everyone must attend the first show, coming home immediately afterwards.
19	Party Privilege	Party privilege is granted on Saturday evening for social gatherings. This includes the permission to remain until 11 P. M.
20	Dinner Engagements	Dinner invitations may be accepted for Friday and Saturday evening. Permission must be secured.
21	Elimination of Recreation Period	When special permission for movies or any social activity has been granted, the recreation period for that evening will be eliminated.
22	Time Allowed For Returning From Functions	For returning from Gymnasium or Carnegie Auditorium—10 minutes. (This includes mid-week basketball games, plays, recitals, etc.) For returning from a party at the Penn Grove Hotel, 20 minutes. For returning from a party at the Armory, 25 minutes. For returning from a party at the Pitt Erie Inn, 30 Minutes. At the expiration of these time limits the door will be locked. Those coming late will forfeit the following week-end privileges.
23	Reporting After Parties	Everyone must report personally to the Dean after parties and be checked off. In case she is not in the lobby for the first comers, they must wait for her.
24	Leaving a Party Early	Anyone wishing to leave a party early is to report to the Dean before leaving.
25	Promptness at Parties	Everyone is expected to arrive at parties before the receiving line breaks up. Good usage require late comers to explain their tardiness.
26	Dancing Not Under College Auspices	Dancing not under college auspices is not allowed.

27 Underclass Girls' Restrictions	Underclass girls may not have mid-week social arrangements except for college functions; games, plays, recitals, etc., after which they must return immediately to their dormitories. In case special permission is granted to go down for refreshments after a game, the time limit is twenty minutes, when the door will be locked.
28 Callers to Leave Promptly	Callers must leave promptly when the lights are flashed.

VII. REGULATIONS GOVERNING COTTAGE GIRLS

1 Cards for Cottage Girls	All girls living in Cottages will come to the Colonial to receive the cards of men callers. Cottage girls are to bring their escorts to Colonial if wishing to have them come in after evening church. No men are to be received at the Cottages any time.
2 Signing Up	Cottage girls must sign up on a tablet which will be provided, upon leaving these cottages in the evening, and cross out when returning.
3 Permission Cards	The Representative from each Cottage must get permission cards for girls wishing permission to go out in the evening. This card must be presented to the Hostess who will return it to the Dean.
4 Promptness	Cottage girls must be in their Cottages at the permission hours specified above.
5 Cottage Girls Under Colonial Regulations	All Cottage girls are under Colonial regulations and will be strictly accountable to the same.

VIII. CONCERNING GUEST PRIVILEGES

1 Frequency	Reasonable latitude is granted in the matter of having house guests. No one is expected to ask for this privilege too often.
2 Good Standing	No one who is under discipline is allowed guest privilege.
3 Introducing Guests	Guests are to be brought to meet the Dean that she may greet them before they are taken into the dining room.
4 Guest Tickets	Meal tickets must be secured before guests are taken into the dining room.

5 Buying All at Once	Meal tickets for all the meals the guest is likely to be present at are to be bought at one time.
6 Refund	In case a guest does not attend a meal which has been paid for, he money will be refunded.
7 Length of Stay	Guests are allowed to stay two nights only.
8 Mid-Week Guests	Mid-week guests are not allowed.
9 Loyalty to Regulations	Both dormitory and campus regulations must be loyally observed during the stay of the guest.
10 Securing Privilege	Permission for guests must be secured before Thursday for the following week-end.

IX. CONCERNING GOING AWAY PRIVILEGE

1 Week-End Privilege	a Three single week-end privileges will be allowed during a semester. b One double week-end and one single week-end will be allowed during a semester. c A single week-end starts on Friday after recitations and ends before recitations on Monday. d A double week-end starts on Thursday after recitations and ends Monday afternoon. e One Saturday to Sunday overnight permission which includes no cuts will be allowed.
2 Holidays	Thanksgiving, Easter, Memorial Day, etc., are not counted as week-end privileges provided one does not incur an cuts. One may leave after classes on day preceeding and return before first recitation on day following holiday.
3 Satisfactory Scholastic Standing	No one whose scholastic standing is unsatisfactory will be allowed week-end privileges.
4 Securing Privilege	Permission for week-end privilege must be secured before Thursday evening. Parents and friends should be informed of this regulation, to eliminate the disappointment of a refusal of the request.
5 Reporting to Dean	Anyone leaving town at any time must report to the Dean imediately before leaving and before going into the dining room upon returning. Failure to comply with this regulation will forfeit the privilege for an indefinite period.

X. CONCERNING DINING ROOM MATTERS

1 Hours of Meals

WEEK DAYS
- Rising gong .... 6:30 A. M.
- Warning gong .... 6:55 A. M.
- Breakfast .... 7:00 A. M.

LUNCHEON
- Warning gong .... 12:10 P. M.
- Luncheon .... 12:15 P. M.

DINNER
- Warning gong .... 5:55 P. M.
- Dinner .... 6:00 P. M.
- Monday Dinner .... 5:30 P. M.

SUNDAY
- Rising gong .... 7:30 A. M.
- Warning gong .... 7:55 A. M.
- Breakfast .... 8:00 A. M.
- Dinner .... 12:30 P. M.
- Supper .... 5:30 P. M.

2 Trays

In case of illness a tray may be secured by getting an order from the Dean. This order is to be given to the hall maid who will attend to the matter.

3 Tray Charge

A charge of ten cents is made for trays. This is paid when getting the order.

4 Remaining Away From Meals

No one is permitted to remain away from meals without either being given permission or, in case of illness or necessity, sending word to the Dean.

5 Guest Tickets

Guest tickets for all meals for which a guest is staying must be procured before taking the guest into the dining room.

6 Prices of Meals

- Breakfast .... .35
- Luncheon .... .50
- Dinner .... .60
- Supper .... .50

7 Promptness

By unanimous vote a time limit of three minutes is allowed to get into the dining room. Anyone coming later than this remains in the Lobby until Grace is said and apologizes after the meal.

8 Obligatory Breakfast

Attendance at breakfast is obligatory with the exception of Saturday, Sunday and Monday. One is expected to choose not more than two of these mornings. Sunday evening supper is also optional.

XI. CONCERNING DINING ROOM CUSTOMS

1 Attitude Toward Waiters	Laughing, joking or talking with waiters is considered to be in bad taste and is not tolerated.
2 Showing Appreciation of Service	It is customary to use the phrase "thank you" whenever circumstances make it natural to do so.
3 Critical Attitude	It is not customary to criticize the food. One need not eat food one does not care for. Remarks are superfluous.
4 Ignoring Accidents	In case of accidents, embarrassment is minimized by ignoring them as far as possible.
5 Conversation	Low toned conversation between two or three, from which others are excluded, is not customary. The conversation is to be general.
6 Conversational Responsibility	Everyone at the table is expected to assume her share of responsibility about keeping up the conversation.
7 Changing Tables	
8 Heads and Opposites	The tables will be appointed as Heads and Juniors as Opposites.
9 Duties of Head	The Head presides.
10 Presides	In her absence the Opposite presides.
11 Reports Absentees	She reports absentees.
12 Maintains Standards	The Head maintains the standards of the dining room.
13 Gives Orders	The Head gives all orders, and sees that reasonable wants are supplied.
14 Gives Signals	The Head gives all signals for beginning and ending the meal. She takes up napkin and silver first; also lays down silver and folds napkins first. The Head naturally assumes the greater part of the responsibility for keeping up the conversation.
15 Leaves Dining Room First	The Head leaves the dining room first.
16 Opposite of the Dean	The Opposite of the Dean follows her immediately into the dining room. In the Dean's absence her Opposite presides in the dining room and is held responsible for maintaining standards.

13

17 Introducing Guests	It is the duty of the Head to see that guest is introduced, though her hostess may make the introductions.
18 Morning Greetings	It is customary to exchange morning greetings upon coming to the table.
19 Grouping	Grouping will not be allowed before Saturday Luncheon and only then when announced by the Dean. If this privilege encourages loud laughing and talking it will be suspended.
20 Manner of Entering Dining Room	Crowding around dining room doors before meals and rushing to places indicates a selfish determination to look out for ones' own interests.
21 Reserving Chairs	Chairs are not to be reserved.

XII. EXAMINATION WEEK REGULATIONS

1 Extra Light Period	Lights will be left on until 11:30 P. M. during exam week. Absolute quiet is required, otherwise the light period will not be extended.
2 Town Privilege	During exam week one may go down town for the usual 20-minute period up until 9:30 P. M.
3 Recreation Period Eliminated	There will be no recreation period during exam week.
4 Movie Privilege	Everyone may have an extra movie privilege during exam week. She may choose the night which best meets her own convenience.
5 First Showing of Picture	It is requested that everyone attend the first show during exam week.

XIII. SUGGESTIONS CONCERNING LEAVING FOR VACATIONS

1 Condition of Room	It is expected that girls will leave their rooms in good order when going away.
2 Forgetting Things	Please do not forget things and so make Mrs. Blair unnecessary trouble.
3 Marking Baggage	Mark all baggage plainly, pasting or tacking labels securely.
4 Leaving Town At Once	No one may remain in town after leaving the Colonial or Cottages unless having been given special permission.

Fill out Change of Address card before leaving the Colonial.

5 Receiving Callers — Men callers will be received and movie privilege allowed on the last night before vacations and the first night following the end of vacations.

XIV. CO-EDUCATIONAL MATTERS

1 Answering Whistles — The card of any man will be refused who offends against good taste by whistling to dormitory girls, talking to them through the windows or in any manner trying to attract their attention.

2 Laws of Hospitality — Men friends will be made welcome at the Colonial at specified times. The "Law of Hospitality" demands that they on their part insure their welcome by co-operating with our observances.

3 Use of Bells — In case a man wishes to see a girl at an unusual time for some special reason, he is expected to ring the bell and send word by the maid that he wishes to see the girl in the social rooms.

4 Use of Wing Doors — Men are not to escort girls to the Wing doors.

If a man escorts a girl to the Colonial he must bring her either to the door opposite Ivy Chapel or the front door.

Loitering at the Wing doors for conversation is strictly prohibited. Special privileges for the following week-end will follow an infringement of this regulation.

5 Time For Cards — On Sunday—Cards are to be in between 7 and 7:20 P. M.

6 To Be Received — On Saturday—Cards may be presented as early as 7 P. M. and not later than 7:45 P. M.

Mid-week—For any engagement, games, College Plays, etc., cards are to be presented not more than twenty minutes before the beginning of the entertainment.

7 Walking With Men — Girls are allowed to walk with men on the main streets of the town. Walking in byways is prohibited.

INDEX
(Continued From Page 2)

Signing Up—Cottage Girls	10	VII	2
Securing Guest Privilege	11	VIII	10
Satisfactory Scholastic Standing	11	IX	3
Securing Week-End Permission	11	IX	4
Time for Securing Permissions	3	IV	1
Talking Out of Window	5	V	19
Tacking and Pasting on Walls	6	V	45
Town Privilege	8	VI	11
Time Allowed for Returning from Functions	9	VI	22
Trays	12	X	2
Tray Charge	12	X	3
Town Privilege (Exam Period)	14	VII	2
Time for Cards	15	XIV	5
Use of Musical Instruments	5	V	20
Use of Laundry	5	V	29
Underclass Girls Privileges	10	VI	27
Use of Assessment Money	6	V	34
Use of Wing Doors	15	XIV	4
Use of Bells	15	XIV	3
Vespers	4	V	9
Week-End Privilege	11	IX	1
Walking with Men	15	XIV	2

16

Appendix D
The Introduction to "The Pilgrims" by Isaac C. Ketler.

Introduction

THIS book covers fourteen years of the history of the Pilgrim Fathers. It is an interpretation of their character and an attempted revelation of the motives which impelled them to withdraw from the Church of England. It deals with the faith which inspired plain English yeomen to undertake a task which men everywhere now regard as colossal.

The story of the Separatist Church, founded by John Robinson and others, is a part of the history of the Protestant Reformation. It is a story within a story. It is the record of the determination of men within the Church of England to go the full length in realizing the highest ideals of the Reformers. These ideals involved entire emancipation from ecclesiastical tyranny and from certain hurtful Romish practices, which the Church of England still retained and enjoined upon the laity. Against all such the early Dissenters, if not openly, then secretly, inveighed. Calvin, and his doctrines, embodied their best thought and highest purposes. In sincere loyalty to God, and the Reformed Faith, they renounced membership in the Church of England, and, acting on what they believed to be a divine prerogative, established an Independent Body, or "Church Estate."

6   INTRODUCTION

What the Magna Charta had merely promised, Calvin and the Reformed Faith fulfilled. The political significance of Calvin's religious creed finds its best expression in the general doctrine of the SOVEREIGNTY of God and the PARITY of men. This was a decided menace to all theories of the *divine right* of kings. To hold Calvin's doctrine was in the highest degree treasonable. Breaches of the Act of Uniformity (in the externals of worship), which Queen Elizabeth had so solemnly condemned, her successor, James the First, was ready to punish with imprisonment, and with death.

The story, as here told, is, therefore, incidentally a defense of Calvin, and his creed. The charge, that the Sovereignty of God bulks so large in the Calvinistic system as to imperil the *freedom of man*, can be sustained only on the ground of very old-fashioned and crude metaphysics. There is no clash between the accepted philosophical concepts of to-day and the fundamental tenets of Calvin. Much of misunderstanding has come of the effort to harmonize his doctrine of predestination with crude and impossible metaphysical notions. Something is also due to a mechanical psychology, which made much of faculty theories, wherein foreknowledge and predestination were treated as distinct and actually separable things, or acts,—as much so, as if they were the operations of quite different organs, or *faculties*, of the divine mind.

It will aid to a better understanding of Calvin's

INTRODUCTION 7

Creed to keep in mind, that neither *fore*knowledge, nor *pre*destination, is a *divine* act. Such acts can be *fore*, or *pre*, to us only, and *within experience*, which experience is, of course, temporal. It will also soften one's natural asperity towards the doctrine of predestination to take into account how really small a factor the human initiative is.

I will not anticipate. *The story, and why given this form*, is the main intent of this introduction. The reader may ask in the language of the Ring and the Book, " Why take the artistic way to prove so much ? " Browning provides also the answer,— " Art remains the one way possible of speaking truth, to mouths like mine at least " ! This is equivalent to an observation of Aristotle's, that the superiority of poetry over history consists in its possessing a higher truth. Certainly one may add, it excels in bringing to the apprehending heart *truths* which the intellect alone will never grasp,—the *essences*, rather than the *accidents* of great deeds, or labours. Why, then, this way ? Because this is the only way to speak the *truth*, that is the *real* truth.

The attempt has been to catch "the breath and finer spirit" of this story. So far as this is realized, it is art, or poetry. I make bold to claim that the interpretation I have given of this heroic Pilgrim-Action does measurably reveal " the breath and finer spirit," that the heart is reached and rewarded in a way unknown to history, or mere prose recital, and that therefore "the artistic way" is justified.

8 INTRODUCTION

The *objective*, that is, the *accidental*, is the relatively little in the story of the Pilgrim Fathers. That which the work-day eye fails to see, that which filters out on the pages of history, and is lost to the heart, is the thing, or essence, of abiding worth in the tale I have attempted to tell.

Beginning with the rise of the Independent, or Separatist, Church, at Scrooby, in A. D. 1606, the story follows the course of the Pilgrim Fathers from their flight to Holland in 1608 to their landing at Plymouth, New England, in 1620.

The book is divided into six parts,—THE FLIGHT (the rise of the Pilgrims, largely at or near Scrooby, England, and their departure for Holland);—THE PILGRIMS' EGYPT (Holland, and especially Leyden, in the times of Prince Maurice and John Barneveldt; the warring religious factions, Arminianism versus Calvinism);—THE PILGRIMS' OLYMPUS (Geneva, and John Calvin's influence; the doctrine of Predestination, and its effect on the Pilgrims);—THE DEPARTURE (the embarkation at Delfshaven);—A TALE OF THE SEA (the Mayflower voyage and the incident of the JACKSCREW);—THE LANDING (the signing of the Compact and the choice of Plymouth).

The book deals with *truth*, that is, with *motives, feelings, aspirations*, not with the objective, the merely *adventitious*. The main action is set forth in blank verse. The use of lyrics, for the most part germane to the progress of the story, is partly for variety, and partly because the feelings found

INTRODUCTION

their expression at times more readily in this way.

During the many years I have meditated this tale I have at no time been able to divest my mind of the sincere conviction, that the Pilgrim movement is the greatest epic-action of the modern world, a theme well worthy of a Homer, or a Milton.

"But is this poetry?" I answer the skeptic,—It reaches my heart, and gives me *truth*, a something which I could not otherwise apprehend, not accidental matters of birth and biography (life, dates and death), but certain vital and deeper motions, as of the eternal spirit of truth, goodness, nobility, God, moving on to a divine goal of victory or triumph. The story, as told here, has this quality (at least for me), not in any one line, or stanza, or book, but in the WHOLE,—the unitary, indivisible march of TRUTH from Scrooby to New England.

I. C. K.

Grove City, Pa., August, 1910.

Appendix E

Isaac C. Ketler

Joseph Newton Pew

Mary Anderson Pew
J.N.Pew's wife and J. Howard Pew's mother

J. Howard Pew

Index

Bible
   department, 51, 72, 73, 91
   infallible Word of God, 8
Calvin, John, 18, 25, 39, 57, 74, 111
Christianity Today, 26, 111
Church of Ageless Wisdom, 159
Coalition for Christian Outreach, 142, 145
College Pastor, 94, 154
Collegian, 72, 81, 96
Combee, Jerry H., 12, 13, 109, 128, 152, 166
Confessionalism, 10, 91, 93, 111
Cory-Thompson, Lory, 79
Cosmogony, 113, 114
Cosmology, 113, 115
Curricular reform, 12
Dayton, David, 9, 46, 48, 74, 88, 89
Diogenes Forum, 163
Edwards, Lee, 9, 48, 72, 106
Epistemology, 113, 115
Exorcism, 160, 161
Foster, Ross, 11, 14, 113, 134, 136, 137, 138, 139, 141, 142, 143, 147, 159
Glenn, Nancy, 36
Graham, Billy, 26, 31, 34, 111
Graham, Sylvester, 78
Harbison Chapel, 2, 66, 74
Harbison, Samuel P., 73

Harbison, William and Ralph, 73
Harker, Stanley J.
   and confessionalism, 91
   changing student manners and morals, 96
   new faculty, 103
   operational and structural changes, 89
   welcomes modernity, 86
Hoffecker, W. Andrew, 6, 14, 38, 113, 119, 140, 146, 167
II Cor. 10
   4 ff, 117
James, William, 114
Jewell, Richard, 168
Jurgens, Bill, 111
Kellogg, W.K., 78
Ketler, Isaac C., 44
   early years in Pine Grove, 45
   education of, 45
   educational programs, 48
   spiritual dimensions of, 52
   The Pilgrims, 56
Ketler, Weir C., 60
   challenges to the College's soul, 68
   education of, 60
   manners, morals, and student behavior, 76
   operational issues, 64
Ketlers, 8, 35, 45
Kingdon, Robert, 18
Knollwood, 21, 23, 24, 34

Kring, Fred
  humanistic, 99
  new style, 97
  underground curriculum, 102
Machen, J.G., 54, 72
MacKenzie, Charles S.
  chapel changes, 154
  curriculum reform, 109
  hiring faculty, 147
  named President, 105
  student housing, 149
  student life, 130
"Man is the measure of all things," 122
Marijuana plants, 164, 165
McEwan, Rev. W.L., 75
McNulty, Paul J., 13, 111, 166, 167
Middle States Accreditation, 66
  report, 89
Mincey, Jeff, 152, 153
Modernism, 10, 38, 69, 70, 71, 85, 91, 93
Moore, John H., 13
Morledge, Richard, 156
Nixon, Richard, 21, 31
Off-campus housing, 143, 149
Ormond, Alexander T., 59, 61
Pew, J. Howard
  appointing Charles MacKenzie, 68
  challenge to "clean up student behavior," 129
  death of, 34
  meeting, 16
  political views, 30
  reflections on, 31
  religious views, 24
  social views, 27
Pew, John, 36
Pew, John Hancock, 36, 38
Pew, Joseph Newton, 36
  entrepreneur, 41
  in general, 40
Pew, Mary Anderson, 67, 218
Pews, 8, 35, 36, 37, 38, 39, 40
pietism, 9, 11, 37, 58, 73, 90
Pietism
  piety, 38, 76
Presbyterian Layman, 20, 26
Presuppositions, 10, 73, 113, 116, 117, 124, 128, 138
Pre-theoretical, 113, 116
Reformed tradition, 8, 18, 58, 111, 113, 114, 116, 141
Religion-Philosophy Keystone, 11
Republic, Plato, 123
Roaring Twenties, 81, 82, 96
Schaeffer, Francis, 137
Soul of the College, 11, 60, 63, 68, 69, 72, 74, 75, 78, 83, 84, 85, 90, 98, 103, 106, 110, 120, 124, 136, 154, 156, 157, 158, 161
Sparks, John, 14, 148, 149, 163, 167
Steen, Peter, 138, 139, 146
Thielemann, Bruce, 155, 156
Thomas, Terry, 137, 141, 146, 147
Traditional historians, 126

Victorian customs, 72
Westminster *Confession*, 9, 40

Westminster *Shorter Catechism*, 39
Worldview, 10

Bibliographic Essay

Sources for this essay are of several kinds: public records, archives, interviews, published books and pamphlets, pictures, and more. There is one more important source—my personal experience living with J. Howard Pew and decades working for the College and later as a Fellow in the Center for Vision & Values.

No attempt has been made in the text to enter endnotes for the myriad sources of information that have been used. On the other hand, great care has been taken to report facts with accuracy. And, at times, a source has been stated in the text, formally or informally. The remainder of this essay will list and discuss some of the more important sources, noting how they fed the narrative.

* * * * *

Since this essay is an exercise in intellectual history, we note first several books that give some perspective on that subject. A general audience will appreciate Allan Bloom's *The Closing of the American Mind* (New York: Simon and Schuster, 1987), which recounts the demise of the use of classics in traditional American colleges and universities. George M. Marsden, a child of, and student of Reformed thought, has written two important books that deeply affect the question of Christian scholarship in America. They are *The Soul of the American University* (New York: Oxford University Press, 1994) and *The Outrageous Idea of Christian Scholarship* (New York: Oxford University Press, 1997). The first book traces the transition of American higher education from a dominant Christian stance to a totally secular one. The second book is a step-child of the first, explaining why solid Christian scholarship—based on Christian presuppositions—is as valid as any other attempt to seek Truth in the Universe. His assumptions are rooted in the same Christian framework as the authors of the College's religion/philosophy course. Indeed, Marsden has spoken at Grove City College several times. Paul Kemeny's *Princeton in the Nation's Service* (New York: Oxford University Press, 1998) should be mentioned here because Kemeny was a student of Marsden and writes about Princeton as a chapter in the history of Christian colleges. W. Andrew Hoffecker's *Charles Hodge: The Pride of Princeton* (Phillipsburg, NJ: P&R Publishing, 2011) is included here because of Hoffecker's focus on Princeton and on piety, a theme noted many times in the present book.

      Other books concentrate on facets of the College's past. It's important to note that no comprehensive history of the College has yet been written. They include an early piece, Lee C. McCandless' "History of Grove City College," a Master's thesis submitted in April 1925. From today's perspective, this piece would be considered a substantial course paper. Weir C. Ketler wrote *An Adventure in Education: 75 Years of Grove City College (1876-1951)* (New York: The Newcomen Society in North America, 1957). The item appears to be an extension of an address Weir Ketler presented in Erie, Pennsylvania in 1927. These items qualify as reminiscences of his time at the College, and seem to be the only formal publications of Weir Ketler. W. M. Ramsay, an English educator, became enamored of Isaac Ketler's work as President of the College during the first years of the 20th century and wrote *An Estimate of the Educational Work of Dr. Isaac Conrad Ketler* (London: Hodder and Stoughton, 1915). The book appears to have had several titles due to several separate printings. Needless to say, Ramsay's book was a very appreciative narrative. As noted in the text, Isaac Ketler himself wrote *The Pilgrims: An Epic Interpretation* (New York: Fleming H. Revell, 1910), which is discussed at length in the text. Its Introduction is also included as an appendix. L. John Van Til's first publication about J. Howard Pew, a pamphlet, was his "The Legacy of J. Howard Pew: A Personal View" (Grove City, PA, Pine Grove Publishing, 1982), written on the occasion of Pew's 100th birthday anniversary.

Several additional books more specifically about the College include the following. Charles S. MacKenzie's "Reminiscences of the Hopeman-MacKenzie Era at Grove City College (1971-1991)" is an extended informal essay that appears in two forms. One is type-written, copies appearing here and there. I have had a copy for years, unsure where it came from. A second copy, in some respects a second edition, is in the College archives, embargoed for MacKenzie's lifetime. He was gracious enough to grant me permission to read it in the archives, after a day-long visit with him at his dwelling in New Wilmington, PA. No doubt, others would be given the same permission. Dale Bowne, a long-time member of the Religion Department, has done the College community a great service by assembling pictures of all the stained glass windows in the Harbison Chapel and then writing a narrative about them. It appears with the title, *Harbison Heritage: The Harbison Chapel Story* (Grove City, PA: Grove City College, 1989). The dedicatory addresses presented in 1931 in the College archives are a treasure as well.

J. Howard Pew delivered dozens of addresses during his long life on economic, political, and religious/theological topics. I had the pleasure of aiding him in writing some of these in his later years. Some are in the College archives, some are in the hands of private parties (I have more than a dozen), and others surely are in the Sun Oil papers. An effort should be made to collect them for further study. This is a good place to mention a small book by Mary Sennholz, compiled a few years after J. Howard's death. Its title is *Faith and Freedom: The Journal of a Great American* (Grove City, PA: Grove City College, 1975). After a brief sketch of his life, she presents a series of excerpts from his speeches, many of them focusing on his economic views. Mary was a skilled student in matters economic.

A handful of more substantial books include the following. Hans F. Sennholz' *The First Eighty Years of Grove City College: The Ketler Years* (Grove City, PA: American Book Distributors, 1993) sees Isaac Ketler as an entrepreneur who really began three institutions before he started the College in 1884. The "entrepreneurial" element is a valid insight, but not the main motivation for Isaac Ketler's work. David Dayton's *'Mid The Pines: An Historical Study of Grove City College* (Grove City, PA: Grove City College, 1971) is still the basis of all subsequent accounts of Grove City College or facets of it. Until someone does a comprehensive history of the College, Dayton's book will stand as the foundation for studies down to 1970. Professional writer Lee Edwards was commissioned by the College to write an account of its past. Edwards published it as *Freedom's College: The History of Grove City College* (Washington, D. C.: Regnary, 2000). He focuses on forces and factors that were affecting American higher education in general as the backbone of his study, plugging into it factors from Grove City College's own past. He built upon Dayton's work and upon many interviews of College faculty, administration, board members, and students. Long-time Weir Ketler-appointed faculty member and Dean of Men/Students Fred Kring, after retirement, published his view of the College and his time there under the title *One Day in the Life of Dean Fred: Autobiography or Legend* (New Wilmington, PA: Globe Printers, 1988). It presents a dissenter's view of the College's development during its time of mid-20th-century reform.

Made in the USA
Middletown, DE
23 April 2015